LEARN HOW TO TALK TO ANYONE

OVERCOME AWKWARDNESS, MAKE
CONNECTIONS AND SOCIALIZE WITH EASE

THE SUCCESSFUL INTROVERTS GUIDE SERIES
BOOK 1

BRENDAN PAUL

GOLD
RIVER
PUBLISHING

INTRODUCTION

There are times I wish I was a master magician so I could disappear into the folds of time, without consequence, without missing a beat. As an introvert, I need so much time to myself. I feel expansive and peaceful in my own space, constricted and chained, when confined to social situations. I can't blossom when pressed against everyone else.
–Jaeda DeWalt

A party! Oh no! Mel thought. *What am I going to do at a corporate party—make small talk with customers I hardly know?* I'd rather disappear into the woodwork than embarrass myself!

A rather odd thought for a guy, you would think? Not if you are an introvert dealing with social anxiety.

Mel shivered inwardly, thinking of the ordeal. And yes, it was an ordeal for him, making small talk, mingling (or rather, standing around), and clutching a glass of bourbon (not too strong) as though it were his lifeline. All the while thinking about escaping—to the confines of his home, where he did not feel pressured to impress, socialize, or engage in animated conversations with people he knew nothing about—all the while sensing their watching and judging him.

Mel was by no means shy or an anxious individual; just that afternoon, he had advised his client about the dwindling stocks they were facing and offered them some cutting-edge promotions to counteract the damage—it was an impressive fact-based talk, but it worked; facts, figures, and in-your-face straight talk with no frills and friendly banter involved. Hence, there was no need for fretting or the dread of speaking to people because he was in his comfort zone.

Mel is smart, funny, and likable—only when he has a purpose and the right people to talk to. But throw him into a room full of strangers and Mel starts to go through a fight-or-flight situation. It's brought on by his dread of casual conversation and being put in the spotlight. Mel's introversion makes him feel like a total outcast like he just landed from Pluto! He knows his capabilities, and among his many talents, casual conversation is not one.

Simply put, Mel is an introvert—like you and like me.

Why Do You Hate Small Talk?

Small talk is feared or disliked by introverts, shy people, and those dealing with a social anxiety disorder.

These are the common causes of:

- Fear of social rejection when attempting a conversation—not being heard when in a group, especially if you are soft-spoken.
- Having nothing in common with total strangers.
- Assuming people aren't interested in what you have to say.
- Having no clue about the art of making small talk.
- Fearing that your conversations will be meaningless.
- Dealing with the exhaustion of socializing, useless banter, and mingling.

These problems crop up due to introverts' strict sense of what they like and dislike and don't want to bother with unless compelled to do so—like Mel having to attend the office party.

A shy person will simply dislike feeling awkward. It's due to low self-esteem. Someone dealing with social anxiety will have several issues on a neurodivergent level, mainly stemming from fear and stress.

Here are some typical introvert codes to live by:

- Small talk is like a barrier that gets in the way of a real conversation; it's pointless, shallow, and fake.
- Despise the big egos that often form parts of small talk.
- Avoid being put on the spot at all costs.
- Socializing zaps energy.
- Prefer relationships with deeper meaning.
- Small talk is a violation of privacy.
- Possess higher emotional skills than the average chatterbox, and are comfortable with themselves.

All these codes mean most introverts are not keen on random socializing; like Mel's presentation to his client, it must be a meaningful exchange and not mere small talk. This is because introverts process everything internally; hence, they need more time than is afforded for a comeback when making small talk. Have you ever woken up in the middle of the night with a witty comeback to a conversation six hours after it took place? Now you know why that is.

Being an Introvert Is Not a Permanent Condition

As an introvert, I want to teach you to embrace your individuality, unless you are already a confident introvert.

You may think you communicate too much when, in reality, you need to increase the quantity of your small talk to fit right in with all the casual chatter that is taking place. It's a matter of letting go and going with the flow. But since you have not conditioned yourself to that type of activity, it is a new skill you must learn.

By the end of this book, you will be armed with skills to avoid being a wallflower or the person that often goes unheard. You will learn to contribute toward useless small talk in a way that makes you feel inclusive in a group of people not interested in the percentage of dolphins that show up on the coast of California every summer, for example.

But I am not offering you a magical quick fix; I want you to understand the history behind the condition you are dealing with—to figure out your fears, insecurities, and doubts and develop self-confidence (that magical elixir for facing any problem) and a sense of your true potential.

It is a step-by-step process that will help you overcome the following:

- Psychological, emotional, physical, and cultural barriers.
- Learn the value and art of listening to what you think is unimportant—a great socializing tool.
- Rules of holding a conversation (yes, there are rules).
- Staying grounded, interested, and casual (without going off-topic and turning light conversations into deep discussions that make others uncomfortable).
- Looking confident—even if you are a quivering pot of jelly inside—because appearance makes a huge difference.
- Learning to read the person you are talking to; nonverbal cues are clues for what's going on inside the other person's head.
- Coming across as "cool," where you don't look as though you are trying too hard to join a conversation.

- Most importantly, I learned the art of building relationships with people.

From One Introvert to Another

How do I know all this?

Like you, I am an introvert, but I have learned to take control of my thoughts, emotions, and behavior to project myself better, more confidently, to be less awkward, and not to come across as a weirdo (the latter begs to differ, though). But weirdness aside, I am a testimony to prove that any man or woman can overcome the challenges of being an introvert and meet people, speak to people they don't know, and form lasting friendships.

I know you want that change, but you are not sure of the "rules," what to say, and how to act so you don't look unconfident and, well, odd. You want to avoid the stares, the blank looks, and even times when your sentences seem to float over everyone's heads and disappear unheard, which sadly makes you clam up and decide not to say anything else. Believe me, I have been through all that trauma—done and dusted.

I want to arm you with the tools I used to overcome my social anxieties to help you easily integrate yourself into society, learn to enjoy the prospect of socializing and making small talk, and let people other than your close friends see the witty, interesting, and fun side of you.

Therefore, in a true introvert style, let's cut the small talk and get down to the subject at hand!

1

GETTING SOCIAL BY KEEPING IT CASUAL

That's all small talk is—a quick way to connect on a human level— which is why it is by no means as irrelevant as the people who are bad at it insist. In short, it's worth making the effort. –Lynn Coady

One of the greatest introverts of all time, Albert Einstein (of course he had to be one), once said, "The monotony and solitude of a quiet life stimulates the creative mind."

And maybe that is exactly the type of philosophy by which you strive to live.

But what about the times you are not thinking about being creative and stimulated? The times you want to relax, let go, and have a good laugh to overcome your anxieties or that tiresomely long day at the office. As an introvert, you may be cool and know exactly what you want, but admit it: Don't you yearn at times to engage in some silly gossip or small talk to wish the blues away?

The beauty of learning small talk is that it does not wait for the right person to come along; you don't need a friend who "gets you," a colleague who matches your wit, etc. You can use small talk anywhere—at the supermarket, the drug store, and so on. I know this because, after many years of isolating myself from informal chatter, I find the activity quite uplifting and a no-commitment kind of therapy for when you need some basic human connection.

This chapter aims to explore small talk and all the introvert taboos associated with it (mainly that small talk is irrelevant). Let's look at those taboos logically and find the loopholes for improving your situation—or, rather, dispelling those taboos to help you find a clearer path and turn the tables on your perception of "small talk."

Small talk can be silly or unimportant conversations that do not tax the mind—light discussions you have with random people that have you smiling inwardly and outwardly; they are healing and soothing to a tired mind. Albert Einstein himself was known for his witty quips and knew how to make light conversation, which means he learned to overcome his social anxieties and his introverted beliefs to benefit from the small talk—and so can you.

Did you know that Michael Jordan is an introvert? One of the most successful athletes the world has ever seen, now turned into a successful entrepreneur. Jordan was loved for being a team player but is also a very private individual. He rocks both roles perfectly, despite being in the spotlight often, and is proof that being an introvert is certainly not a handicap.

He is a "non-anxious" introvert who, despite loving his privacy, can manage to rise to the occasion when needed. This is what Michael said, and I believe it is an excellent motivator for what we are trying to achieve.

My attitude is that if you push me towards something that you think is a weakness, then I will turn that perceived weakness into a strength. –Michael Jordan

Defining the Difference Between Social Anxiety Disorder, Introversion, and Shyness

You may feel confused about being an introvert, a shy person, or dealing with a social anxiety disorder. So, let's take each condition step-by-step.

Introversion is not categorized as social anxiety and has clear-cut differences; let's explore them:

Social Anxiety Develops Over Time, Introversion Is Inherited

Genetics plays a starring role when it comes to both introversion and social anxiety. Although, for the latter, society, lifestyles, and circumstances play a huge part as well. Let's say the straw that breaks the camel's back: If you already possess anxiety traits, you can be *pushed* toward developing social anxiety, whereas your introversion is most likely hardwired into your genes. For example, my friend John's father was a soft-spoken, quiet individual who also had a strong personality, which made him a great role model, especially for John, as I found he inherited the same characteristics, preferring a quieter, more fulfilling lifestyle.

Your experiences are the main cause or contributory factors for developing social anxiety, for example:

- As kids, we are constantly put under scrutiny and expected to perform, measure up, and outshine. Were you made to feel as though you needed to be more social, more outgoing, or smart, just like your mom's best friend's daughter? They are factors that make you feel put under the radar of your family, society, friends, or peers—factors that make an otherwise shy and awkward individual develop social anxiety because they live under the pressure of being judged and scrutinized, thus developing a mindset of never measuring up to society's expectations.

- Being the victim of a bully is another factor that contributes to social trauma, leading to low self-esteem and a lack of confidence that affects your social skills.

- Avoidance is the third factor that causes social anxiety. How many times have you left an official function as soon as the speeches were done so you didn't have to hang around for small talk? Or the times you decided to call in sick and apologize for missing the party because you were just too anxious about meeting people and making small talk? Or even the times you decided to bury your nose in your smartphone as a means of escape and avoidance for times you felt awkward or shy? They all sum up to avoidance syndrome, which in time develops into social anxiety because you are encouraging and feeding your insecurities instead of facing them. Facing those problems will help you realize that socializing is not poison and is not as scary as you imagine it to be. Instead, you end up with a phobia of socializing.

In contrast, an introvert does not avoid out of fear. They have simply decided that socializing is not their preference. A confident introvert will prefer a quiet meetup with a few friends to a room full of people at a party where they feel out of place. For the introverts, there are no overcoming fears; it's simply a matter of changing their mindset and fine-tuning their socializing skills, such as becoming better at small talk.

Dealing With a Social Anxiety Means You Fear Being Stripped

Bare

Let's recall that dream many of us have at some point in our awkward lives—well, at least I did—the one where you show up in school or to work stark naked. You feel violated and exposed, and your not-so-pretty parts are revealed.

That is exactly what someone dealing with social anxiety fears—all their flaws being revealed. No, not that big, ugly wart on their behind. But that perceived flaw about themselves they carry around like a huge weight.

It can be many things that they fear people will notice about them: The way their voice falters and cracks when they're having a conversation, their cheeks getting flushed and red, or the fact that they are not witty with responses and even get tongue-tied. Such perceptions are their own creations, notions their mind has formed without a realistic base. Therefore, they will be surprised to learn how little it matters to other people or how much of that behavior goes unnoticed. Unfortunately, in the mind of the socially anxious individual, those are huge flaws they strive to protect from being revealed.

But an introvert's perception of being revealed is different; an introvert that is not socially anxious, like Michael Jordan, will not harbor the fear of having flaws revealed. In their minds, there is nothing to be revealed. It's a case of, "This is it; I'm not good at small talk, so I will avoid social circles." There is no anxiety involved about being stripped bare and left vulnerable under the scrutinous glare of strangers. They tend to avoid things they feel they are not good at.

The Desire to Be Perfect and Social Anxiety

Perfectionism can drive you crazy, especially if you are highly critical of yourself! The need to be well and perfect, and avoid being evaluated negatively by others is a tough order to live up to.

The woman who has the perfectly maintained house when visitors drop by unannounced; the guy in the office with a flawless track record of no blunders; meeting deadlines on time; never arriving late; having the ideal kids with the best grades and the perfect behavior (no kid is going to agree to that); there you have it, examples of the high standards we set for ourselves and believe others expect of us. The truth is, we expect it of ourselves, and so we deal with the anxiety and pressure that follow, trying to be seen as perfect by society.

The introvert, in contrast, will not be so finicky about their performance. They will stutter and struggle at making small talk or even socializing in a group of people, but they are not dealing with the pressure of being excellent or perfect, and their reward is not what others think of them but their own self-satisfaction at perhaps rocking a conversation, which sadly does not happen often, and so they avoid circumstances where they feel they will be put under the radar.

Introverts Know What They Want, the Socially Anxious Fear They Can't Keep Up

Albert Einstein, when he made that speech about monotony and solitude stimulating the creative mind, was comfortable with who he was and what he wanted. He was a socially secure introvert who could hold a witty conversation when he wanted but preferred solitude over socializing. And so, introverts will leave a party early because they prefer to unwind at home, watch a movie, and relax in their comfy home.

The socially anxious person, on the other hand, is wracked with fear and doubt; they avoid a party or even leave early because they think they don't fit in, they will not be missed, they are boring, etc. They are not confident enough to say, "This is what I want: solitude, time in front of the TV, a hot dinner, and a good comedy." Instead, their insecurities and self-doubt activate their fight or flight mode, and they decide to skulk away quietly and nurse their doubts, fears, sadness, and so on in despair and alone.

Now, do you see the differences between being introverted and developing social anxiety?

A social anxiety syndrome can be healed, but it needs deeper analysis and attention to detail in order to start healing. You need to heal because it is a condition that has developed over time and is not a part of your character, like being an introvert.

A study conducted on the subject proved that harboring extreme fear about being judged by others in a social situation can lead to a lowered quality of life, unstable relationships, isolation, and even depression (Wang et al., 2022).

You can attach skills to your introverted nature—the art of making casual conversation and learning to appreciate small talk, and its therapeutic values—to enhance who you are. You cannot change your introverted character; that is part of your genetic code, and really, you should be comfortable with who you are. But you can get the add-ons by making a few adjustments. But the question remains, "Can you be a socially anxious introvert?"

Let's explore this further:

What Is Shyness?

Being socially awkward, feeling nervous about social gatherings, and experiencing discomfort when interacting with people are all symptoms linked to shyness. Negativity is the main cause here, since shyness often occurs due to the following factors:

- Making a negative evaluation of oneself.
- Being overly self-conscious.
- Being overly preoccupied with a negative self-image.

A shy person will feel nervous about attending a function where they have to meet new people, make small talk, face the sales assistant in the shop, or when someone unknown approaches them to chat.

If you are shy, you will display the following characteristics:

- Common physical traits include blushing (do you feel the blood rush to your cheeks when you are talking to a group of people?), a racing heart that you sometimes fear is so loud that others will hear it beating, and excessive sweating.
- You are worried about how you project yourself— *they will think I'm a complete nerd*—similar thoughts have you doubting your social skills.
- You also possess a negative self-image. *I'm just too boring.*

Adolescents are often shy because they have yet to develop a sense of self, which starts to take shape closer to leaving their teen years. Since social skills are undeveloped in shy people, it's not considered an inherited trait, although shyness can stem, in part, from possessing a demure character.

Shyness, therefore, is based on both genetics and experiences. Children not exposed to socializing will be less outgoing and more reserved, but as they grow, leave home, and expand their encounters, they will overcome their shyness. Due to these factors, shyness is not thought of as a social anxiety disorder.

Say Hello to SAD

Social anxiety disorder (SAD) is not to be confused with introversion, shyness, or the simple awkwardness that we all experience at some point in our lives. SAD is a condition that develops over time; no one is born with social anxiety.

On the contrary, an introvert will most likely inherit their traits. But it is a fine line, and sometimes the boundaries between social anxiety and introversion can merge. Hold on, though—don't go diagnosing yourself as a socially anxious introvert just yet. Let's review the facts and put them in order because, to fix a problem, we need to figure out the root causes and get updated on some background information.

What Is Social Anxiety Disorder (SAD)?

SAD is more than feeling awkward or shy. It's a type of anxiety disorder that compels those dealing with the condition to feel fear and anxiety when they feel they come under the radar and get scrutinized, for example, in the following situations:

- Job interviews.
- Dates, talking in front of a crowd.
- Dealing with a sales assistant at a shop/supermarket.
- Eating meals in front of other people.
- Even using public restrooms.

The fear stems from the dread of being judged, facing rejection, and humiliation. The symptoms associated with SAD are similar to those of shyness or introversion, but the root cause and severity are more intense.

Symptoms of SAD

- Physical symptoms of excessive sweating include increased heart rate, jitters, upset stomach, shortness of breath, and blushing.
- Your body becomes stiff, and you feel awkward, plus you talk very softly.
- The mind goes blank; you will think of a witty reply to the conversation, perhaps a few hours later.
- Feeling sick to my stomach.
- Feeling extremely uncomfortable being around strangers at a social gathering.

- Inability to make eye contact, and it is almost automatic to look away instead of smiling. Most people who do this under the influence of SAD regret the action.
- Avoid going places where they must interact with other people or be in a crowd, especially walking into a room where people are already seated.
- Finding it difficult to return an item to a store.
- Feel very self-conscious because of the perception that they are being judged and will be seen in a negative light.

Can you associate any of these symptoms with any other conditions? You must consult a professional if any of these symptoms are holding you back from interacting with people, and you fear you are starting to live a life of isolation. We already discussed experiences and factors that lead to social anxiety. Now let's look at factors within social anxiety that prevent proper communication.

How Does Anxiety Lead To Bad Communication?

Your brain plays a major role during a conversation. In fact, it gets very busy when it comes to communication. One part of the brain must pay attention to what you are hearing, and the other part of the brain must form appropriate replies. After all, if your brain played no part in conversation, you would reply, "Another piece, please" to a question of "How was your exam?"

Anxiety and Brain Fog That Causes Bad Communication

Mental health issues are a leading cause of brain fog, and SAD is no different. Brain fog does not mean your brain is not functioning as it should; it simply means your thought process is disrupted due to external causes, for example:

- Inability to concentrate within a conversation: This happens when your mind is distracted and you cannot focus on what is being said. Instead, your mind wanders across several thoughts, or it may dwell on one particular thought that has nothing to do with the conversation taking place. This type of distraction takes place regardless of the type of conversation, be it casual or more important.

- Distorted talk occurs when you are anxious, and your tongue does not function as it should. Generally, your tongue moves automatically to form the syllables needed to make words, but when you are nervous, that auto-response may get hindered. This causes you to stumble over words, which adds to your awkwardness.

- Nervousness induces overthinking: Being cautious and thinking about every response hinders the natural flow of the conversation. Casual talk is all about well-being. When you overthink your answers, there is an awkwardness that prevails, and the people you are talking to can pick up on those vibes and feel a discomfort within the conversation, which is probably why you sometimes feel as though people think you are not interesting.

- Panic: This is a common trait when you are dealing with any form of anxiety and is quite a disruptive factor. Panic can create brain fog and block your natural thought process, where you don't register what's taking place because you are dealing with a fight-or-flight impulse and all you can think about is getting away and the fear of rising nervousness.

- Inability to listen: All of the above factors cause distractions not only in your response—your brain is so busy dealing with the panic, fear, etc., that it fails to help you listen to what is being said. You become so focused on trying to *read* the nonverbal signals in the other person because you are so anxious to know their judgment of your nervousness that you totally fail to focus on the words coming out of their mouth. This is one factor that leads to low self-esteem and harsh judgment of yourself because you focus so much on deciphering body language that you miss the words, which are a more accurate account of what the other person is thinking.

How Can I Avoid the Pitfalls of Bad Communication?

Before we discuss therapies that help with social anxiety, here are some tips for overcoming the above stumbling blocks in a conversation:

Do Not Try to Hide Your Anxiety

Surprisingly, a lot of people can tune into your anxiety, and not everyone is as judgmental as you think them to be. Besides, trying to hide your anxiety is in itself traumatic, and will increase your anxiety. Something I always find works is to explain myself, i.e., "I'm sorry, but my mind was somewhere else. Would you mind repeating what you just said, please?"

Even on days when your tongue has decided to take on a life of its own, it's okay to say, "Oops, my tongue is tripping me up today; please just bear with me."

Such statements take away the trauma you would otherwise face while dealing with embarrassment and trying to hide your panic. Admitting you're dealing with difficulty is much more freeing than trying to cover it up. Keep in mind that no one is perfect, and everyone is dealing with personal turmoil.

Do Not Be Harshly Critical of Yourself

Avoid judging yourself and agonizing over what you just said or did. Overthinking can cause a lot of unwanted damage.

Of course, it's in our nature to overthink and analyze our moves; it's a hard habit to break. But through conscious practice and accepting your flaws as part of who you are, you can avoid the stress of overthinking and trying to maintain the illusion of the perfect you.

There may be times you are engaged in a conversation, but a part of you seems to be standing on the sidelines, watching and judging every time your tongue gets tied or you struggle to come back with an appropriate reply to a question. That is your critical self-interfering with your flow of thought and preventing yourself from a fully immersive experience of the conversation that is taking place.

Use positive statements or affirmations to help you over-come your low self-esteem and become more accepting of yourself. Choose to repeat these statements several times a day, and they will help you break your habit of overthinking and being overly critical of yourself.

Here are some simple yet powerful affirmations that you can choose to recite daily to help you stop overthinking in the negative:

- My mind will not dwell on destructive thoughts.
- I have control of my thoughts, mind, and behavior.
- I am strong, and I love myself.
- What I think is not my reality.

Get in Some Experience

To become better at conversation, you need to practice. Find ways to build your conversation skills. Meet a friend for coffee and start an interesting, *no-holds-barred* conversation to see where the flow takes you. Make sure you open up and allow yourself to feel comfortable talking more than you normally would. You can even use a mirror at home to practice speaking up, learn to project your voice more confidently, smile, and make yourself interesting and animated.

Dealing With Social Anxiety on a Professional Level

It may not be easy to seek professional help for social anxiety. However, if you are at a point where the condition has taken over your life and is interfering with your relationships, and you face extreme fear and anxiety at the thought of socializing, talking to strangers, or even going out in public, it's best to seek help from a qualified therapist.

Here are the types of therapies used to treat SAD:

- **Cognitive Behavioral Therapy (CBT)**

This is one of the more successful methods of treatment for SAD. CBT is used to treat a variety of anxiety and depression syndromes through several different techniques. Therefore, make sure to identify a therapist experienced in using CBT specifically for the treatment of SAD.

CBT works by helping you change your cognitive behavior, or rather, your thought process that leads to problematic behavior. The methods adopted are designed to reduce your panic and help you feel more in control of your thoughts, mind, and behavior. Think of CBT as a technique to help rewire your brain and turn negative thoughts into positive ones.

CBT addresses the following that is hardwired into your brain:

- The negativity you harbor leads to low self-esteem.
- Showcasing perfectionism as unrealistic and helping you cope with critical overthinking.
- Stressing over the past, accommodating guilt, anger, or embarrassment.
- False ideals that other people are constantly judging your actions.

The therapist will use CBT sessions to coax a self-discovery response from you that helps you come to a realization and face truths about your limits and capabilities, which helps build self-worth. CBT works on the premise of dedication and constant practice. Unlike introversion, dealing with SAD is more intense, and simply telling yourself to change your way of thinking is not going to help. You need to initiate a change in your thought process one step at a time through repetitive exercises and behavior.

- **Exposure Therapy**

Exposure therapy is a part of CBT and is a gradual process that exposes you to a specific fear. While exposure therapy is generally conducted by a trained therapist, there are methods you can use on a daily basis to help you overcome your social anxiety fears.

Avoiding a particularly traumatic situation will only lead to an acceleration of that fear. Gradual and prolonged exposure to the stressful situation will help you to overcome it and realize, over time, that the threat was not as severe as you had envisioned it in your mind.

Exposure therapy works to help overcome several social phobias associated with SAD, including:

- Fear of eating in front of other people.
- Fear of socializing.
- Talking to strangers.
- Using public restrooms.
- Public speaking.
- Fearing conflict and not speaking up.
- **Group Therapy**

Group therapy is also a cognitive behavior treatment that

works by addressing the main fear of someone dealing with SAD—the fear of socializing and speaking to strangers. However, with group therapy, you are meeting with and discussing your problems with people dealing with similar conditions. It's a freeing experience that offers comfort in the knowledge that there are others out there dealing with your same anxieties and fears. Plus, people in group therapy are extremely sympathetic and understanding of your condition, and will offer you some of the best advice for working through your social phobias.

The Importance of Sleep When Dealing With SAD

Among all those therapies out there, a good night's sleep can work wonders toward helping you deal with social phobias. A rested and alert mind is more capable of paying attention to a conversation and is less likely to react negatively.

Do you often spend your nights tossing and turning in bed, wondering about that last conversation you had or how you could have avoided embarrassing yourself?

I wish I hadn't stumbled over my words and made a fool of myself. Or, if only I had come up with a witty answer to make everyone laugh instead of standing there looking glum.

These thoughts, which often have you imagining worst-case scenarios, can keep you from getting a good night's sleep, as do most anxiety-related syndromes. Studies have proven that poor sleep is more prevalent in people with social anxiety, and those same people went on to face a less successful day impaired by heightened panic and distress, which probably kept them awake yet again.

The same study identified a lack of stimulus in the part of the brain that enables social interaction among the people identified as dealing with a social phobia—bad sleep makes socializing seem like a bigger threat than it did before (Buckner et al., 2008).

It gets worse because further studies proved that those

dealing with SAD, when experiencing a lack of sleep, were more reluctant to engage socially, thus triggering a desire for isolation and loneliness (McLay et al., 2021).

So how do you get out of this vicious cycle of poor sleep-related social anxiety?

While therapeutic treatment can be left to the professionals, you can help yourself to enjoy a good night's sleep and see people as less of a threat. Once you start trying out techniques to manage your social anxiety, it's important to make sure you improve the quality of your sleep at the same time.

Tools for Encouraging a Good Night's Sleep

Decompress at the End of the Day: Meditation and Journaling

A lot of your restlessness stems from your anxieties, i.e., your mix of panic, fear, and embarrassment that you endured throughout the day. Decompressing before bedtime allows you to come to terms with your thoughts, emotions, and actions. The following are some excellent techniques:

- Meditation: Find a quiet spot and sit down or lie down in bed. Take five deep breaths; inhale through your nose and exhale from your mouth to the count of five. To become more accepting and less judgmental of yourself, try reflecting on your day's events as a form of meditation. Analyze, but less critically; leave yourself a margin for error; and overlook perfection—there is no such thing as the perfect social interaction. Look at your interactions and fears from a fresh perspective. For example, if you shied away from talking to a stranger you met at a party, ask yourself what you could have done differently to overcome your phobia of interaction.
- Journaling: This may not appeal to everyone, especially men, but it is a proven tool for

overcoming fears and doubts associated with
anxiety. Journaling is about transferring the fears
and doubts associated with a mood in your head
onto paper or any other outside source—a
document on your computer, for example. That type
of shift clears your mind and helps you see your
anxieties in a less foreboding light. Besides, you
don't have to write poetic prose if you don't want to,
and a simple word or sentence that would define
your mood at the end of the day will be enough, i.e.,
angry and embarrassed.

There you said it; you are feeling embarrassed, hence you
are angry—with yourself or someone else? Now write, or
doodle around the word, the causes you think contributed to
that mood. Why were you embarrassed? Once you put those
reasons down, they may not seem like huge problems, and that
mood could lose steam. More importantly, they will not cause
you anxiety or a sleepless night. If you struggle to find a reason
for your mood, don't push it; leave it and engage in another
activity that helps your mind to settle. Watch a comedy sketch
on TV, read a book, or go for a walk to clear your mind before
bedtime.

Establish a Set Bedtime Routine

Maintain a good bedtime habit by establishing a set sleep
and wake time. Do not deviate from this unless you have an
important function to attend that you can't get out of solely on
the excuse of missing your bedtime.

Go to bed and wake up at the same time every day; that way,
you are programming what we call our circadian rhythm (CR)
to follow a healthy routine. Your CR is your sleep-wake cycle,

and it can be fine-tuned to follow a set routine. A healthy CR is what defines us as wholesome adults.

Prepare for Bed

I don't mean brushing your teeth and getting in your PJs; prepare for bed by winding down and signaling your body to get ready for sleep. Read a book or engage in a light exercise routine about an hour before bedtime to work out your anxieties. Physical exertion is a good way to end the day, as it helps tire the body and soothe the mind. When your body is exerted and ready for rest, it will not support your analytical mind on its midnight escapades, and you can enjoy a good night's rest.

Eat Healthy to Maintain a Healthy Mind

A healthy diet is key to many of our life's problems, and it certainly aids the anxious mind. Here are some healthy habits to maintain the well-being of your mind, body, and soul:

- Include plenty of protein in your breakfast. Protein-rich food helps stabilize your blood sugar levels and keeps you feeling fuller for longer, thus avoiding hungriness and mood swings that can impact your social behavior.
- Include carbs in your meals. Serotonin is your feel-good hormone, a neurotransmitter secreted by your brain and gut. Foods containing carbs help trigger the release of serotonin, which can impact your mood and your response to social stimuli. However, too much protein in the meal can block this effect. Therefore, make sure to maintain a healthy balance of both carbs and proteins in your meals. For example, a breakfast high in protein can be followed by a lunch that is carb-fueled.
- Strive to eat a balanced diet, including omega-3 fatty acids or fish oil. Omega-3s contain eicosapentaenoic

acid (EPA) and docosahexaenoic acid (DHA), which are essential for brain and eye health.

- Stay well-hydrated because dehydration can reduce energy levels. Did you know that most of your organs contain water? Your brain, for example, is 73% water (Water Science School), and when dehydrated, the organ cannot function at its optimum level, which is when you feel that zap in energy—low energy often leads to mood swings, which is one reason you tend to avoid casual talk and interact with other people.
- Consume alcohol in moderation. Yes, I know that a glass of wine or a drop of whisky may give you the courage to speak to that interesting-looking stranger, but when you are dealing with a neurodivergent condition (where the brain has evolved and works differently from others), it is best to avoid stimuli that inhibit the function of your brain. Alcohol can make you feel more nervous and also inhibit sleep. It's not a magical elixir that instills courage. And the same goes for coffee: Too much is never a good thing.

Building Your Self-Confidence to Overcome Social Anxiety

The constant fear of thinking you are under surveillance and being judged and criticized makes it hard to let go of your social anxiety. But let me tell you a little secret: Most people are too preoccupied with their own problems to spend time judging you; it is your own mind that acts as judge and jury, instigated most of the time by a lack of self-confidence.

The following are my tried-and-tested methods for building self-confidence and socializing with renewed faith in yourself:

Be Your Biggest Fan

The key to building self-confidence is to become accepting of who you are, flaws and all. Attain satisfaction within yourself by staying true to your limits, skills, and experiences. A large chunk of your social anxiety stems from your lack of self-worth; therefore, learn to appreciate yourself.

Use your journal (or doc if you prefer a more technical approach) to make a list of your special qualities—even the most inconsequential ones. Try to establish a connection with your true self, not who your critical mind perceives you should be. If you are a quiet introvert who prefers to hang out with his best friends on a Saturday night instead of club hopping, accept that person and don't stress yourself about not being an outgoing chatterbox. Stay grounded about who you will help overcome most of your social anxiety fears because you are not stressing over *not* being that person.

Squash Your Fear of the Unknown

Do you dread attending a social event that you know nothing about? How ritzy is the event going to be, what type of people will attend, and will you fit in? These are some of the thoughts that will randomly float around your mind. That is the fear of the unknown, so what do you know? You take away the element of the *unknown*.

Prepare for the event by arming yourself with some information to dispel your nervousness. Check out the venue, ask about the type of food on the menu, and also get the guest list so you can prepare ahead and be dressed appropriately to match the people you expect to meet. Taking away any element that can lead to you feeling awkward will help dispel your fears and nervousness.

Learn to Adjust to Sudden Change of Plans

Despite getting updated on the event taking place, there are going to be a lot of unexpected events that you must mentally prepare for. Prepare your mind by telling yourself that unexpected outcomes are not to be feared and are a fact of life.

Let's say you plan to show up at a social event, say a few "Hello's," have a bite to eat, and leave before the main event is done before the socializing commences. However, your plans may not work out, and you may get roped into staying for some friendly mingling. Don't let your anxieties take over at these times; instead, go with the flow, and who knows, you may find a group of people you can relate to and end up having a rewarding conversation.

Project Confidence

Body language can reveal more about yourself than what you are saying. This was a discovery made by Dr. Albert Mehrabian. His 7/38/55 rule is based on his research, which he says confirms 7% of communication is projected verbally, 38% via your tone of voice, and 55% through body language (Park & Park, 2018).

Based on these findings, the solution is simple: Project yourself confidently. Talk in a tone that is audible—don't mumble, make eye contact, and stand up straight. Projecting your self-confidence thus will not only make others see you as confident (even when you're not), but your actions will also instill a sense of self-confidence.

How to Tackle Various Social Events: The Best Conversation Starters

The art of making a good first impression by talking to a stranger with ease and holding up your end of a conversation are not magical skills some people are born with—well, maybe some are—but you can learn them with a bit of practice, patience, and loads of confidence.

The following are some tips on starting a conversation at different social gatherings:

Parties and Dinners

You can shop for that snazzy outfit, shower, make sure you

look your best, and check your breath too. But once you get to the event, how confident will you feel?

You may be a confident introvert who has not felt the need to practice casual conversation much. All good, except for when sudden curve balls pops-up like a party or dinner.

The following are some techniques to practice for your next *social* event:

Take a Chance and Make Contact

Whether you are shy or an introvert, don't hang around like a wallflower waiting for someone to talk to you. Chances are, most other people are feeling as apprehensive as you are and will find it odd to communicate with someone who is not making eye contact. Make eye contact; if a room full of people seems intimidating, choose two or three people to do so.

Stop overthinking and take the plunge. Once you make eye contact, do not look away; rather, smile. That's your invitation to say "Hi." Whether your initial gesture to make contact is rejected or does not matter, chances are you will hook up with people you have more in common with.

Start With a Casual Introduction

If introducing yourself is the most difficult part, practice at home. There is nothing wrong with fine-tuning your introductory skills. Head over to the person once you make eye contact, smile, and say, "Hi, I'm... It's nice to meet you. What's your name?"

If you are addressing a group of people, don't focus on just the cutest girl or guy there; include everyone and say, "Hi, I'm... How is everybody doing?"

Ask a Few Interesting Questions

Take the standard question, "Where do you work?" "Where do you live?" etc., and make them a bit more creative, for example:

"How has your day been?"

"Are you from around here?"

Prepare ahead and maybe jot down some interesting questions you could ask the people, depending on the event you are attending. Do not take along cue cards; simply memorize the questions.

Listen, Await Your Turn to Speak Up, and Don't Judge

The rules for making casual talk are simple: Ask a question, listen, and do not be overly judgmental. Don't ask someone what they like about New York and then proceed to override them by telling them what you like about New York or act fidgety when someone is talking to you. Listen attentively; don't smile at someone else over their shoulder when the person you are talking to is telling you about their sick dog.

Mirror what they are saying through your facial expressions. That is a show of respect, and you will garner a friend in the talker when you make an effort to listen and ask follow-up questions, such as, "Oh, so you've started working in New York this year... how interesting do you find it?"

While listening and asking questions, do not become overly judgmental of what is being said. If the other person strikes up a political conversation, don't turn it into a debate. Nod and smile, even if, in your mind, you disagree with what's being said. Don't attempt to take the conversation to argument status. Keep casual talk casual.

Be Tactful, Be Patient

The real art of conversation is not only to say the right thing at the right place but to leave unsaid the wrong thing at the tempting moment. –Dorothy Nevill

Speak your mind, but navigate any sensitive subjects with care. Wait your turn to speak your mind, and when you do so, simply add your opinion; do not make it a challenge or your personal declaration of war.

"I certainly don't agree with your opinion, but I believe Jasper should've never been made president!"

Instead of the above, you could be more tactful:

"I hear you, but I guess some of us have different opinions —each his own, though."

Change Up With Care

We introverts are pretty confident with the types of people we like, so in case you get stuck at a party with a person or group of people you don't really click with, make a tactful exit. Don't look bored and slowly wander off; rather, end the conversation politely by having someplace to go:

"I think I will get myself a bite to eat. It was great chatting with you, and I hope everything works out."

Coming up With Interesting Topics to Speak About

Do you know how some people have lots to talk about? For example, what they did, where they went, and what they wanted to do—you simply stand there, racking your brains for something interesting to say about yourself, and all you can think about is the great deal on toilet paper at Walmart you remember.

Here's the thing—to talk about yourself, you need to establish a sense of self. Remember when I told you to be your biggest fan? Find your sense of purpose, your dreams, and your ambitions. Maybe get out that notebook (also known as your journal) and try jotting down some future targets you want to meet. Create a spreadsheet of dreams and goals. Once you start to live a full life, you will be surprised at the anecdotes and experiences you have to talk about.

Want to get a bit *sciency* with your conversation skills? Nothing too complicated, but a few excellent *conversation rules* that really help we introverts define the art of making casual conversation and nail it!

2

THE SCIENCE BEHIND CONVERSATIONS

And surely one of the best rules in conversation is, never to say a thing which any of the company can reasonably wish had been left unsaid. –Jonathan Swift

If one word could describe Alicia's approach to casual talk, it would be "safe." She would follow all the rules, listen attentively, smile, look shocked, and nod her head all at the appropriate times, but the moment the other person stopped talking, she made a gesture of "over to you." She would freeze, and nothing more than an "mhmm... yeah" or "oh, I see" would leave her mind. Her mind would go blank, or she would have simply lost interest and stopped following the conversation—a surefire way to kill a conversation; Alicia knows it, but she can't help it. That is as far as her casual conversations will take her, unless the other person graciously makes an excuse to get away to find a more interesting counterpart.

What if I told you there are rules and techniques you can follow in coming up with excellent replies and conversation material?

Let's approach the conversation in a scientific manner; let's break it down so that you can look at the many elements that go into a successful flow of casual talk. It's not rocket science, though; it's simply a leg up for we introverts to be able to see the importance of each component involved in making a conversation successful. They are components you would have overlooked and never fine-tuned because, let's face it, casual conversation was not on your list of priorities—until now.

The Essential Components of Casual Conversation

Every conversation is made up of important components that help with the flow of chatter, your understanding, response, and control of the direction the conversation is taking. Doing so will instigate a better response from the other person and maintain the element of interest, which I believe is the most important component within a conversation that flows with ease.

GIVING OUT INFORMATION:

The Introduction

Before you dive right into a conversation and start asking questions, it's important to give out some information about yourself, thus making yourself more accessible and approachable to others. We introverts can often be wrongly perceived as standoffish and unfriendly simply because we are more private and less outgoing among strangers. Giving out information about yourself is a good start to dispel that myth (I call it a myth because I know inside most introverts is a warm, sensitive person who struggles to let others know they are approachable). However, since we are private people, giving out information does not mean exposing too many of your personal details. For example, no one you just met wants to know that you are allergic to cheese. Keep it simple, talk loud and clear, and introduce yourself—your name, where you are from, and any work or connection you have to the host or event.

The Descriptions

Giving out information is clearly not linked to just your personal details. Here is the most vital part of the conversation that leads to interaction between you and the other person on any given subject, and this information must be divulged clearly if you want to hold the interest of the other person.

- Speak up in a clear and precise voice (but don't sound condescending or *like you know it all*).
- Make the conversation more animated; throw in a few metaphors and examples you have to help the other person understand what you are talking about.
- Don't go into professor mode; use simple language and avoid technical phrases. If you talk about how beautiful the Prunus serrulata is in full bloom, most people will imagine a complicated plant from the Stone Age. But say cherry blossom trees in Japan (aka Prunus serrulata), and you will get nods of interest.
- Give out information in small, easy-to-digest chunks; don't talk so fast that you stumble over your words and give out too much information that tips the conversation towards boredom.
- Be clear about what you are talking about:
- A validated point.
- Your view of an argument, in which case it would be factual.
- For a proposal you want to make, have your facts straight as to why you are saying so.

- Be alert and observe; if no questions are asked, chances are you are not being very clear, or your explanation is too complicated.

The Details

The crunch when it comes to a conversation is how much information to give out. On a personal level, keep it limited; no one wants to know too much about the person they just met. If you are discussing a particular subject, be precise and as accurate as you can be. Avoid talking about points you are not 100% sure of, and you can avoid the dilemma of being called an exaggerator or purveyor of false information.

Asking: The Engaging Component

Show your interest in the other person by asking them engaging questions. Setting the pace for the other person to talk about themselves is always a hit, and you are sure to garner interest and favor points.

There is a small twist to the plot here because, by handing over the reins of the conversation to the other person, you are empowering them with the feeling of being in control of the talk when, in fact, it is you who are manipulating the conversation in the direction you want it to flow. Of course, nothing too sneaky; it's simply a good method to help the other person feel at ease in your presence and take the conversation onto a friendlier, more casual level.

Asserting: Whether Right or Wrong

Being assertive when communicating will help you boost your self-confidence. It's considered a core skill to master for effective communication and one that makes people sit up and take notice of what you are saying or the opinions you are expressing. If you value standing up for yourself and your beliefs, you must learn the skill of assertiveness in a conversation.

Most people, when conversing, will use assertive statements, which are statements made with confidence and finality. Someone can be assertive whether what they are saying is the truth, a fib, or something they don't have accurate details about. Sometimes people may lie on purpose in the hopes of creating a favorable impression or for a specific reason. While I do not condone lying, there are times a white lie can save a conversation.

The Art of Proposing to Make a Conversation More Interesting

This is one of the best components to master if you want to know the art of keeping a conversation interesting. When you propose within a conversation, you are opening the door for the other person to respond and dive right into the conversation. It's similar to encouraging them to talk about themselves, except that this time you are getting more input on a specific subject in which everyone can be a participant.

Here are some guidelines for making a proposal within a conversation:

- Put out ideas and opinions; be open to suggestions and further opinions:

"I thought last night's NFL game was a good example of how effective strategies can be game changers. Did you catch the game? What do you think?"

- Propose an action:

"Maybe the patio would be a good place to sit down with our drinks and enjoy this discussion."

- Helping the other person find a solution to a problem they are discussing:

It's unlikely that someone you are having a casual conversation with is going to want to discuss their family problems, but there are times people will talk about an immediate or casual problem. Maybe an office colleague will want to talk about unfairness at the workplace, an issue with a friend, or a minor health issue they are dealing with. At such times, you can take the conversation to a more personal level by offering some helpful input that will help the other person come up with a solution or maybe help them better understand the situation.

Use "qualifiers" within a conversation to open up a pause from which the other person can take charge. A qualifier is the opposite of being assertive but can help the flow of a conversation, especially when you are proposing.

Common qualifiers that indicate to the other person that you may not be assertive or sure about a suggestion and are therefore open to suggestions are words such as perhaps, maybe, and could (we, you, etc.).

Example: "Perhaps you will be able to explain more about the subject than I can; would you like to take over?"

Helping Yourself to Stay on Track and Focused by Summarizing and Checking

Summarizing goes hand in hand with paraphrasing and is an effective tool for staying connected within a conversation. Whether you are indulging in a casual conversation or sitting in on an important presentation, summarizing can help.

- Summarize by recapping what you said, especially if it was a lengthy discussion and bulky divulging of information.
- Summarize what you just heard to clarify and confirm everything you heard. Doing so is letting the other person know you have been paying attention and understand what they said. It also encourages them to continue with the conversation. Have you noticed how some people suddenly stop

talking and find an excuse to walk away? That happens when they suddenly realize you are not really paying attention, and other than a chatterbox, no one likes to have a one-sided conversation.

- Check in-between summarizing to make sure the other person has understood what you just said. That way, you won't be wasting steam on someone who is going to nod blankly and find an excuse to walk away. Checking works both ways because, as you summarize what you heard and understood, it's good to check that what you heard is correct.

"So, you mean it took a whole three hours just to make it to the start of the trail?"

Summarizing and checking is a good way to help you and the other person remember the gist of the conversation, which eventually leads to other questions, proposals, comments, and so on, making the entire interaction interesting.

Build a Conversation to Give it More Body

As an introvert, you know how difficult it is to sustain a fragmented conversation that keeps jumping from one casual topic to the next until you and the other person run out of questions to ask and random information to give out.

When you build a conversation, you give it body, structure, and added elements to go further, thus avoiding those stunted and awkward comments.

You can build on what you are saying by coaxing the other person to dive right in with responses, replies to your arguments, and theories of their own. Building a conversation will even work when your mind is a total blank and you are stuck with what to say.

Example: "I do believe this bad weather we are experiencing is a part of global warming, or I could be wrong. What do you think? Have you heard anything about how long this hot spell will last?"

You can even take what the other person is saying and build on that conversation, preventing it from fizzling out.

"You mean the weather is a fluke and will change soon? Are you looking forward to that, or do you like such warm weather?"

Think of building a conversation as a form of bonding that instigates combined thinking between a group or two people. I believe it's the ultimate conversation saver.

Including: Building Your Group

I often feel more comfortable conversing with a group of people than struggling to form a conversation with just one person. If you are the same and you find yourself stuck trying to make small talk with one individual, call in the reinforcements.

Include others and send them the signal to join. You can stand at an angle, making sure to leave gaps within the circle to let others join. Be alert to who is within earshot, make eye contact, smile, and send some random comments their way, for example:

"We were just talking about that last speech by Stephen; did you find it insightful as well?"

Deliberately including others and widening the circle of people builds on the conversation and also helps the discussion go further.

Watch out for body language. If someone outside your circle is turning their body toward your group, keeps looking your way, and pays attention to what you are saying, it's a signal they want to be included in the group.

It's also an act of empathy to include those feeling left out into a group you are in, but watch out for the above body language because there are also people who stand just outside the circle but do not wish to be included, are interested in other conversations, or are simply not focused on a discussion.

Excluding: Information and People

Sometimes we need to keep conversations and the exchange of information private. On how many occasions have you been engaged in a private conversation with someone only to have a third party interrupt you and stop the dialogue?

What do you do at those times?

- Be short and curt with your answers. Send out signals to say, "Please leave; this is a private conversation."
- Don't acknowledge their input—comments, advice, etc.
- Use negative body language; turn away from the person you want to avoid.
- Be straightforward and polite, for example: "Elisabeth and I were having a private chat; if you don't mind, please give us some privacy."

I would suggest using these strategies if the private conversation is urgent and cannot be postponed for the sake of politeness. If you cannot expect diverse reactions from people, not everyone will take being excluded with grace.

Tips for excluding information from a conversation:

- Have ground rules; know what you are going to discuss and what's off the table.
- Focus on your main discussion and ignore any comments or questions that you wish to avoid.
- Conversation topics do drift, and when that happens, tactfully bring back the focus to the subject that needs to be discussed.

Use these focus tactics when you need to discuss a particular subject and stay on course.

Avoiding What is Uncomfortable

Similar to excluding information, there are some topics that must be avoided in casual conversation. Talking about politics or religion, for example, may seem interesting among like-minded people, but in general, such topics tend to make people uncomfortable. Avoid them, including the subjects of sex and violence, unless the group you are with starts a discussion on them. Even so, do not jump right in; observe everyone's reaction to the subject, and if you notice anyone looking uncomfortable, tactfully change the subject, and you will be appreciated for doing so.

How to avoid uncomfortable topics:

- Ignore any reference made to them.
- Offer vague replies, look away, and act uninterested.
- Change the subject.
- Wave off the topic as unimportant. It offers no details, and you should not ask for any.
- Be straightforward and express your desire to avoid taboo subjects.

Example: "I really am not interested in the subject." Or "Let's talk about something else."

Blocking Someone in a Conversation

Learning the art of subtly blocking someone within a conversation is a skill that will be handy at times. It's quite close to avoiding topics you are not comfortable discussing.

Here are several options for blocking people:

- Ignoring and avoiding: Do so by avoiding questions the other person throws into the flow of your conversation. "But what about..." Ignore these types of questions and continue with the flow of your conversation.

- Diffuse—you can tone down a rather hot topic that threatens to go off course by trivializing the comments. Make a joke of the comment, or try reducing the intensity of it by giving the comment some attention and then moving on to a different topic.
- Take a rain check—one way to politely ignore a question or comment is to take a rain check. "I will have to check on that and get back to you."

Feel Comfortable to Disagree

To feel confident and comfortable during a conversation, you need to exercise freedom of speech—within the boundaries of tact and politeness, of course, since we cannot go around telling people exactly what we think of them, not all of the time anyway.

Disagreement is a healthy factor that helps you stay focused and interested in the conversation. Disagreements will range in degree from simple debates to major arguments. But keep your discussion down-to-earth, taking the other person's feelings and opinions into consideration.

"That's a good point, Brian, but I must disagree; let me explain why."

We already covered assertion as a factor in casual conversation, and when a person is making assertive statements, it becomes difficult to agree because they are already passively expecting 100% agreement from everyone included in the conversation.

On these occasions, it's best to let them finish, wait for a pause, and then gently raise your argument or explain why you disagree.

Remember, not everyone will react kindly to disagreement; they may ignore your remarks or even ridicule you for not understanding.

Stand your ground if the subject is important, but keep the following in mind:

- Practice diplomacy when disagreeing if the person is an important contact you need to maintain. Find an excuse to exit the conversation and avoid further conflict.
- Use careful, tactful phrases to put forth your argument. This makes it easier for the other person to react kindly to your comments and consider your point of view.

Drawing Attention to Yourself

Have you ever rolled your eyes (inwardly, to yourself) at what someone was saying?

Most likely, that person was talking about themselves in a rather casual but manipulated manner that makes them look phenomenal—that is, using the element of self-promotion within a conversation.

To most introverts, drawing attention to oneself must feel as though they are placing themselves on the sacrificial altar, but there is a positive aspect to self-promotion.

Most conversations are power struggles. Each person is trying to project themselves in a positive and *awesome* light.

Here are some sample statements:

"My company, which I formed from scratch, is one of the few recognized for innovative marketing strategies, so I may be able to offer you some tips."

"In my opinion..."

A person into self-promotion will listen to what the other person is saying impatiently before interrupting to reply with a bigger and better option of what they did, similar to what is being discussed.

"Oh, that's nice. The 2-mile run sounds like it was fun. I

myself did a 6-mile run last year and found it very invigorating."

While this type of talk may veer very close to the boundary of boasting (oops), there are times a tad bit of self-promotional talk will do you well. However, keep in mind that while trying to build credibility, you may forget yourself and lose the entire gist of your self-promotion. Avoid doing so by being aware of responses, body actions, and reactions in others.

When first getting into the act of casual talk, you must be prepared to endure this type of conversation from other people; it is a general practice that governs most conversations.

Use self-promotional talk

- when sitting for an interview.
- meeting someone you wish to impress.

You may not like self-promotional conversations, but you can use such situations to your advantage. A self-promoter loves praise and adoration and will often fall prey to flattery. They will be grateful to you for your kind words, and in return, they will be more compliant and agreeable to your proposals and suggestions. Therefore, listen and observe to help turn the conversation in your favor.

Defending: Supporting Your Arguments

There are times your arguments or proposals will be blocked or challenged by others; defending your statements at those times takes some skill.

Here are my tips for doing so:

- Slide in your proposals—never go into a conversation with an argument. Build it up to the crucial point, then slide in your proposal.

Instead of saying, "Let's plan to go to a movie next Friday."

You can say, "We have all worked so hard these past few weeks; let's plan something fun, like maybe a movie."

- Justify: Always have enough information to back up your arguments and proposals. Without rationalization to back up your argument, you become open to attack, which can sometimes happen even if you explain yourself. In those instances, it becomes a personal battle, which you must learn to handle with dignity instead of letting your emotions take over.
- Remain polite: No matter how much you are pushed, keep your cool and remain positive. Always maintain an air of professionalism, and you can't go wrong—no matter how annoying the argument becomes.
- Be accurate when quoting: Let's say you are arguing a point with the other person, and you suddenly bring in reinforcements in the form of a quote made by your opponent on social media, etc. In this case, be accurate and do not stretch the quote in your favor. Avoid being proven wrong and then getting ridiculed and losing face with others.
- Have a strong argument: Do not enter a debate unless you have a strong argument. Without it, you will be tempted to use untruths, which, when debunked, make you look bad.
- Do not turn a defense into an attack: Trying to make sure your argument is not attacked by putting the other person on the spot will turn your defense into an attack because you are adding an element of demand to your argument.

Example: "Oh, come on now, don't argue with me to try and make me look bad."

Understanding Why People Argue

Being an introvert makes you more observant of what's going on by tuning into the other person's body language and perhaps mentality. It is a helpful skill for dealing with different types of conversations.

Here are typical reasons why people argue:

- Struggling with a low self-image. Often, people will be focused on justifying themselves and proving their point if they are dealing with low self-esteem and emotional inadequacy. This makes proving the rationale behind their point important and helps with a lack of confidence.
- Using attack to diffuse. Some people will attack another to distract them from the present flow of conversation. When attacked, the person making the speech will go into self-defense mode and forget the gist of their original argument, which often leads to the conversation taking a different course (success for the attacker).

Now that we have discussed the elements of a conversation, how do you amalgamate them into a decent conversation without offending, coming off as too aggressive or inquisitive, boring, and so on? You follow the rules, of course.

Rules of Conversation

These rules are almost a summarization of all the elements of the conversation we just had.

1. **Know how to seem interested:**

Do so by asking the correct questions:

- Get the other person talking about themselves—a favorite subject.
- Ask questions that matter to the other person. Don't talk to someone about growing vegetables if they live in an apartment.
- Ask questions in the positive sense, not "Don't you just hate it when he is always late?" That is a negative conversation starter and projects you in the same negative light—a turnoff for some people.

1. **Avoid awkward statements in a conversation:**

"I really like keeping to myself and avoiding people."
Even if it is the truth, too much information can stop a conversation. Choose your revelations carefully.

1. **Be Tactful:**

"Did you have a rough night, or were you unwell? You look tired?" Hold your tongue and avoid asking tactless questions. Say something nice or nothing at all.

1. **Be real:**

Showing fake interest in someone is often transparent, and you can't hold the illusion for long. Pay attention and be interested in what the other person is saying, and they will be more open to continuing a conversation with you.

1. **Don't have an avalanche of questions:**

Don't make yourself look like a robot by asking a series of questions. Give the other person time to answer one question before moving on to the next.

1. Avoid arguments:

Try to keep the conversation amicable, even if you strongly oppose what is being discussed. Remain calm and do not instigate an argument; walk away if the talk becomes too much to ignore.

1. Show respect:

Everyone is entitled to their views and beliefs. Be respectful of the other person you are talking to; do not ridicule, dismiss, or treat them as inferior.

1. Be accepting of others' ideas:

So, if you don't like what the other person is saying, that does not give you the right to be overly critical. Don't try to analyze everything the other person is saying. Not everyone likes a *smarty pants*, even if you do know better.

1. Compliment:

Build up the other person's self-confidence. Make them look good and offer praise where it's due.

10. Be open:

Talk openly and share your ideas and thoughts. Do not be so open that you create arguments or offend people. Instead, join in the conversation with your genuine thoughts and enjoy yourself.

1. Don't hog the conversation:

Don't be the person who talks incessantly while others slowly wander away from you or try to avoid getting stuck in a conversation with you. Remember to pause, no matter how excited you are about discussing the evolution of rocking chairs. For example, give others a chance to get in their versions and ideas.

1. Don't interrupt:

No matter how exciting you think your story is, wait your turn. Don't interrupt the other person's talk to get in your opinion—that's downright rude.

1. Accept that people are different:

If you love using humor in a conversation, you may be a tad bit disappointed to find the other person is deadpan and serious, and your funny comments go unnoticed. On the other hand, you can discover that you become popular with someone who finds your jokes amusing and cannot stop laughing. A casual conversation with strangers can take on different dimensions due to the different natures of people. Understand and learn to adapt to the situation, and it will be easier to converse with different types of people.

1. Don't go off-track:

When discussing a subject, try to stick to the main details. Avoid wasting time on unnecessary details. For example, when telling someone about the exceptional dinner you enjoyed at the new Italian place, don't wrack your brains trying to remember at which table you sat.

1. Avoid self-promotion:

Don't talk about yourself in hero mode all the time. If it is a story that requires one, generalize the hero and include others as well as yourself.

Let's Learn to Construct a Conversation

How do you take all these elements and rules and put them into a genuine conversation that works?

A conversation consists of different phases, steps that go from a simple "hello" to a more immersive and interesting discussion. Before we go into the five stages of conversation, it's important to discuss the tools we use for conversing with other people.

- Your voice is the most important. It sets the stage for what you are saying. Since you first bawled your head off as an infant, you have learned to manipulate the tone of your voice. Use that skill in a conversation. A clear and slow tone makes your words comprehensible to others. Create drama (I think of this as the background music to what I'm saying) by lowering or raising your tone.

Use your voice to animate the conversation and hold the attention of everyone in the conversation circle.

"... and so, we ended up lodging at this tiny hostel in Nepal, halfway up the mountain; it was very pretty, until suddenly "boom," there was a huge landslide..."

- Your facial expressions are the backup. Do not try to carry on a conversation or stand in a group listening with a blank stare. It makes some people uncomfortable, and others think you are probably the serial killer they spoke about on the news. A smile or a simple look of interest will increase your mileage and help you break into a circle of people enjoying a good talk.

The Five Stages of Conversation

When we feel awkward entering into casual talk, it helps to go through these five stages:

1. Initiation
2. Preview
3. Business
4. Feedback
5. Closing

Stage 1: Building Rapport—Initiation

Make eye contact, smile, and stand close facing a group of people talking. Let them see you are interested in what's being said. If you wish to start a conversation with a single person, break the ice by smiling at them and nodding your head in a gesture of "hello." If they return the gestures, that's your cue to walk over and initiate a conversation. For most introverts, this first stage is the most difficult, but practice makes perfect. Practice your initiation in front of a mirror at home: a warm welcome smile, a slight nod of the head, and eye contact. Remember to keep these gestures natural and not forced.

Stage 2: Exploring the Field—Preview

Once you break the ice and get over the initial jitters of making contact, you can launch into conversation mode, but keep it simple.

"Hi, I'm John. It's nice to meet you. Is this your first time attending this type of conference?"

We introverts like to get right to the point and not beat around the bush, but during casual conversation, you cannot dive right into a sensitive topic. Instead, you must build up the conversation, be observant of the other person's mood and emotional responses, and then, when you feel it's safe, you can take the conversation to the next level.

For example, let's say you want to join a protest campaign

against environmental pollution, and you finally meet one of the main campaign leaders. Don't start with, "Can I join your next protest campaign?" but rather create a preview, for example:

"That speech on the impact of environmental pollution was quite an eye-opener."

Make small talk and build enough empathy to make the other person feel comfortable talking to you about their personal business.

Stage 3: Get Down to Business

Once you have made enough small talk and shared information about yourselves and you both feel more relaxed in each other's company, you can get down to business and discuss the nitty-gritty of what you need to know. This works even if you don't have a specific agenda and have simply met a person you find interesting and want to know more about their work.

Or, if you simply want to enjoy a stimulating conversation, use this stage to identify the other person's plans, goals, and interests and show interest to help them see you are on the same page, for example:

"Oh, yes, I followed your last campaign and thought it was well planned out; it was a huge inspiration for me since I strongly believe in conserving our planet... and I would love to join your next campaign."

Once the stage is set for discussion, you can go into a more detailed exchange of information and ask what you need to know.

Stage 4: Mutual Understanding—Feedback

Feedback, as we discussed under components of a conversation, tells you if you have been understood and if you are making progress with the conversation. Feedback reviews the gist of the conversation over and over to help keep to the point of the topic and also for you to show empathy and understanding of what the other person is saying.

Remember that showing empathy and mirroring the other person's concerns is an integral part of a successful conversation; for example:

"I totally understand your frustrations; keeping your campaign strong must take a lot of work and sacrifice on your part."

Stage 5: Ending the Conversation—Closing

Once you have achieved goals on either side, the conversation can be closed. Whether you were after more information, you helped the other person air a concern, or you simply enjoyed a stimulating exchange of information, every conversation must come to an end before it gets to that awkward stage of "done and dusted," but we are still here.

Use the same body language and signals as you did in the initiation stage. Smile, nod your head, and indicate you enjoyed the dialog. Take a step away from the other person, turn your body away, and subtly prepare to say goodbye.

You must also catch on to cues sent by the other person—things they may say or do as indicators they wish to close the conversation:

- They may stop asking more questions.
- Use phrases such as "Oh, that's good information; just one more thing..."
- Looking away from you while talking or even looking at their watch.
- End with a simple, "Okay, it was so nice chatting with you; I hope to meet you again soon."

You could ask the person for a contact number if you wish to discuss further business but do not push it if they seem reluctant. Do not show your disappointment; end the conversation on a positive note.

Next, let's discuss some of the more important problems we introverts face in a conversation—barriers. How do you overcome sudden blocks and halts that stunt a conversation and leave you grappling for an escape line? The answers are in the next chapter.

3

CONVERSATION BARRIERS AND ROLLING OVER THEM

Conversation about the weather is the last refuge of the unimaginative. –Oscar Wilde

With so many innuendos about conversations about the weather, I often find myself avoiding the topic, even if I just walked through a storm to get to a party. But avoiding topics about the weather is not the chief problem we introverts face when it comes to stunted conversations.

The dreadful block where your mind goes blank, and you keep thinking, "Now what do I say?" is casual conversation's biggest nightmare. What if I told you that you were responsible for setting up those barriers? It's true!

- fear
- anxiety
- assumptions you make of others

These are the main culprits, or influences, that create barriers in casual conversation. And you need to overcome these concerns and biases to become fully immersed in a conversation, understand the true meaning and intentions behind what's being said, and enjoy a natural flow of dialog between you and the other person.

If your mind is biased toward the speaker and you are dissecting every word they are saying and looking for hidden meanings, you are not really following the conversation, nor do you understand the true meaning of what's being said.

You stand there feeling defensive, misinterpreting, or drawing the wrong conclusion because the conversation is filtered through these influences, which makes it difficult for you to form a connection with the other person.

Three Rules for Engaging in an Unbiased Conversation

Avoid conversations with a mental block by overcoming these barriers.

Do Not Become Defensive; Accept Criticism

"Maybe this wording can be rephrased a bit to sound more enticing to the buyer?"

If you heard this from your manager after you worked hard on creating a sales campaign line, you might automatically go into defense mode.

"His one goal is to put me down and make me look bad—he never respects my work."

These may be some of the thoughts filling your head. They block you from seeing the bigger picture and being open to valid suggestions.

The above example can be experienced in different aspects when the element of criticism enters a conversation to sting your mind and make you defensive.

Be open to criticism; avoid considering it a personal attack that you must prove to be wrong at all costs. When you allow your pride to be hurt, you miss the purpose of what's being said —in this case, advice to make the campaign stronger.

Do Not Draw the Wrong Conclusion

It's simple: If you cannot accept criticism or see the bigger picture, you are going to draw the wrong conclusion. Instead of hearing advice, you hear attacks, and that, unfortunately, blocks the main goal of what the other person is trying to reach with your help. Be neutral; do not be quick to form opinions. There is always an "Okay, you may be right..." to every suggestion you hear. Never let pride create a barrier.

Be a Good Listener

Hearing is the process of receiving sounds and tones that create stimuli. It's a biological process where vibrations enter your inner ear.

On the other hand, listening is the act of paying careful attention to what is being said and using your temporal lobe. Located near your temple, it deals with listening comprehension, memory processing, and emotional regulation.

You need to use this process to be a good listener and not simply *hear* what is being said. Most introverts are passive listeners, which means they listen to a conversation but do not contribute; it's a negative trait that you are in the process of trying to overcome. But you can use some elements to your advantage, and that is the act of passive listening to properly comprehend what's being said before jumping to conclusions and offering hasty replies or simply shutting down and going blank.

Exploring Barriers That Block Casual Conversations

Apart from ego, fear, and wrong perceptions, there are external and internal factors that cause conversation blocks. Let's explore.

Emotional and Psychological Barriers: Your Negative Perceptions of People

Emotional barriers are responsible for you being biased toward the speaker and forming wrong opinions.

What leads to emotional barriers?

- Bad experiences: Dealing with emotional anxiety and all the baggage that comes with the condition is a factor. Whether your fears stem from past experiences or are the result of interference from other people, it does not matter; those negative emotions create mistrust and act as barriers that prevent you from forming an unbiased connection and correctly hearing what the other person is saying.
- Low self-esteem: This makes you fear the judgment of others and worry about their perception of you. Social anxiety aggravates your feelings of insecurity, which automatically become a barrier, stopping you from successfully interacting with others and enjoying a fulfilling conversation.
- Negative emotions: Emotions are psychological barriers that influence how we react within a conversation. If you are stressed or angry, for example, your level of patience will be low, and let's say you are stuck in a conversation with a self-promoter, chances are you are going to walk away or indicate your impatience, forgetting all the tactful measures we discussed when it comes to dealing with a similar situation. Emotions like anger can cause you to say things you may regret later and to misunderstand what the other person is saying.

Physical Barrier: Body Language and Proximity

Body language is an integral part of the conversation, and sending the wrong signal can often result in you creating a negative impression on the other person. Looking away (as an involuntary reaction to your shyness), not reducing the distance gap, etc., are all physical blockages that prevent a conversation from taking place. Luckily, they can be overcome through conscious effort.

Attitudinal Barriers: How Your Character Interferes With Conversation

Your attitudinal barriers are based on your attitude, of course, and assumptions. Unlike emotional influences, they are not a result of circumstance but are built up over time due to external and internal factors. Your cultural background, as well as your social standing, have a greater influence over your attitudinal barriers that are based on professional and personal elements. They, in turn, create egotistical and judgmental attitudes. They prevent you from settling into a conversation and trusting and understanding situations in a rational way.

Perception Barriers: Dealing With Mental Blocks

Not being able to see eye-to-eye is another conversation barrier. When you are unable to come to an understanding with the other person, the conversation has no path forward and will lose steam.

Cognitive biases prevent you from hearing and understanding accurate versions of what the other person is saying. What this means is that you are dealing with a mental fault that interferes with your ability to judge and make decisions fairly. Biases are designed to help us make quick decisions, but when a mental judgmental error occurs, you develop cognitive biases. The error is a kind of short circuit that takes place in your comprehension process, which is brought on by social pressure, stress, and a lack of emotional regulation.

Prejudices: Hanging On to Cliched Ideals

Having stereotypical policies and attitudes creates biases that interfere with your ability to settle into a conversation. Instead of actively listening to what is being said, someone with a prejudice will hear a preconceived, toxically filtered version of what's being said.

Cultural Biases—When Your Traditions Get in the Way

Different cultural beliefs and languages can sometimes make casual conversation difficult. While one culture may teach openness and the importance of forming connections, another will promote privacy and the concept of giving people space. Hence, differences in beliefs and dialects can often be a barricade that prevents people from varied cultural backgrounds from wanting to socialize and interact with others.

Socio-Religious Barriers: When Obliviousness Holds You Back

A lack of proper knowledge about different religions can make religious fanatics avoid wanting to interact with those of a different faith for fear of their beliefs and ideas in connection to their own religion. These doubts and clashes of ideals lead to a partition that prevents some people from actively engaging in conversations with people who have different ideals or represent other faiths.

Not Sticking to Simple Language

"Hi, I'm Sean, and I'm the head of the methodological subdivision for the principle-reactor chamber." This is the type of sentence that will garner a few smiles and some blank looks.

Instead, saying, "Hi, I'm Sean. I'm the head of the tech division for the main generator room..." will certainly garner a few interesting looks and questions.

Don't use complicated jargon in casual conversations; keep it simple. People will know if you are smart even if you don't use big words.

Nail Small Talk and Overcome Conversation Barriers

Overcoming your casual conversational blocks will help you to evolve as a person because, in doing so, you will be overcoming long-standing stereotypical ideals, fears, anxieties, and other character traits of introversion that stop you from being more outgoing and social.

Aim to start with a simple "Hi" rather than "so, what's your story?" This is a rather bold approach for we introverts, but it opens up a wide scope of possibilities and places you in the driver's seat of small talk with loads of confidence.

Have Your Objectives and Ideas Ready Before Communicating

To overcome introversion when making small talk, you need to be confident, and to look and feel confident, you need to know what you are talking about. Even small talk must have depth; you must speak clearly and in an understandable manner with enough information to back up what you are saying.

Small talk is not about saying, "This drink is really nice."

You are not aiming for a full stop; instead, you need a comma, a pause, from which you or the other person can continue to add body and depth to the conversation and make it interesting.

"I decided to cut back on the new renovations because of the rising cost of roofing material, which is going to skyrocket by the time we get to the end of our project in three months."

"Have you done any construction recently?"

Be Mindful of Your Audience

You may be a professor of aeronautical science, but if you are attending your kids' parent-teacher meeting, you cannot go around talking on the level of your qualifications as though all those parents there are your work colleagues.

Be observant, get a feel for the audience, and make small talk relevant to the person or people you are interacting with.

Include Everyone in the Conversation

I often end up feeling more comfortable with one or two people in a circle of conversation and sometimes end up addressing and looking at them when I talk, regardless of whether the others are listening to my speech.

Avoid singling out people in a circle of small talk, and make sure to lock eyes with everyone there to show inclusion. That way, you are encouraging everyone to contribute and participate. Remember, the more, the merrier when it comes to small talk.

Be Mindful of Your Tone: Language and Topics

Avoid using complicated jargon; match the audience and their interests. Be mindful of your tone; use it to animate your talk and avoid taboo topics.

Make Sure Your Talk Is Relevant to the Audience

Don't try to talk about something you are familiar with if you feel it's inappropriate for the audience or person you are chatting with. You don't need polite nods, a stifled yawn, and a hasty retreat.

You may know the ins and outs of indoor plumbing, but if you are talking to an artist at his gallery, he may not be interested in the latest U-bend pipes to fit any drain. So, use your intuition and pick on fragments of what you heard about building a decent conversation topic that's relevant to all. Even asking questions about what the other person does will help you stop talking about what's familiar to only you.

Don't Roll Over Topics

Some people have a habit of flipping through different topics in a conversation without a clear indication of changing subjects.

"How was the weather in Bali?... The last time we visited Toronto, it was pretty cold."

So, the person you are talking to was in Bali, and you visited Toronto. If you had waited for a reply and then added your Toronto bit, the message would have been clear; instead, you probably have people confused and disinterested—project messages clearly. Skip topics after a clear indication that you are doing so, and always wait for a question to be answered before jumping to the next.

Be Positive and Assertive

Successful small talk is centered mainly on projection; never enter one by mumbling something incoherent—not everyone has the patience to try and understand you. Be positive, look confident, and speak clearly to convey a message of confidence in what you are saying.

Practice Quiz for Communication Problems

Are you ready for a test?

USE this worksheet to practice and analyze your responses to different situations:

1. Your work colleagues invite you to join them for evening drinks, but you decline. But one says, "You should be more of a team player instead of avoiding all social events."
What do you say?
2. You're at a party surrounded by a group of strangers when one person says to you, "Are you okay? You look bored."
What do you say?

3. At a client's meeting, you presented a project you worked hard on, but they say, "I want to make a few changes."

What do you say?

4. You meet your partner's friends for the first time, and one says, "Tell us about yourself."

What do you say?

5. On board a flight, the person next to you says, "Are you on a solo holiday? This is my first time vacationing without friends."

What do you say?

6. You give your aunt directions to get to a certain place, but she looks confused and says nothing.

What do you say?

7. You get back to work after vacation, and your boss says, "What did you do over the summer."

What do you say?

8. Your partner says, "Why do you keep working at that place? If it were me, I would have quit already!"

What do you say?

9. You ask your friend to meet you for a movie, but they say, "We always do the movie thing. Let's try something different for a change."

What do you say?

10. You're at an office cocktail party, and your colleagues surround you and say, "You always leave early. Why don't you hang with us today?"

What do you say?

Next, we are going to focus on active listening. The most important component of casual conversation is *listening* to what the other person is saying. Let's explore the various components of listening, the qualities of a good listener, and all the skills you need to follow a conversation and be an active participant in small talk.

4

PRICKING UP YOUR EARS

Listening is a magnetic and strange thing, a creative force. The friends who listen to us are the ones we move toward. When we are listened to, it creates us, makes us unfold and expand. –Karl A. Menninger

Have you experienced the magic of a brilliantly told story?

The skill of being able to narrate a coherent story can open many doors and opportunities for you. Stories are how we let others know what's going on with our lives, how we impress to gain, and how we form lasting bonds with others by revealing ourselves as vulnerable.

If you ever *aced* an interview, achieved the title of "best salesman of the month," or won the speech contest in college, you know the importance of a positive, clear, and convincing narration.

But first, listen before you begin to speak.

The success of telling a good story lies not only in the narration but also in how well that story is received by the listener. You can talk about your adventures climbing Mount Everest all by yourself, but if the other person pays no attention, you will gain no mileage from that story, no matter how skillfully it is narrated. Therefore, listening is a form of narration, and the two need to work hand in hand for success.

To be a good storyteller, you need to be a good listener, because listening to the stories of others is how you learn empathy, form a connection, and become an immersed or active listener who understands more than the words they hear. You learn to read between the lines, read body language, forget biases, and see the talker in a new light. And as you listen and learn, you are filing away information for times when you have a story to tell in all its animated glory.

Effective Communication Starts With Listening

Did you know that during a job interview, while they are listening to how well you answer the interviewer, they are also looking for signs you possess a "soft skill"—the skill of listening?

This is because being a skilled listener is highly valued in the corporate world. Employers see good listeners as employees who are able to take on projects successfully and understand daily tasks with ease. Such people are good at giving coherent speeches, resolving conflicts, and forming strong bonds with their colleagues.

Deconstructing the Process of Listening

Hearing sound and accurately interpreting what's being said is the act of listening. We already covered that certain biases on the part of the listener can warp what they hear. When you listen actively, you comprehend what the other person is demanding, asking, offering, or proposing. It's a skill that will help you pick up on essential tidbits to join a casual conversation among strangers. It's also a skill that will help you in the workplace, at home, and so on, because active listening teaches you empathy.

Since a vital trait for introverts is a sensitivity to others' moods and emotions, listening is a skill you can easily fine-tune. Proving this point, there are studies that confirm introverts possess the skills to be highly social, a skill that gets undermined because of your tendency to shy away from socializing. However, by becoming more outgoing, you can build your self-esteem, and that will help you lose your inhibitions about socializing and use your natural talents of empathy to easily bond with strangers (Tuovinen et al., 2020).

What Are the Types of Listening?

"Elizabeth, there is a shortage of seats up front; could you please move up a space and make room for Mark?"

Take the above statement, and it will go through the following process:

RECEIVING:
Focus on hearing and deciphering sounds.

⇩

UNDERSTANDING:
Deciding on the meaning
of the message and its
relevance to you.

REMEMBERING:
Putting your
listening skills to
the test to retain
what was said.

EVALUATING:
Your perception of
the method and
your biases come
into play here.

FEEDBACK:
Responding to the
statement.

- If Elizabeth listens accurately, she will hear the message for what it is: "Please make some extra space."

- If she is emotional and listens through a bias, she will take it as a personal insult: "Move aside to make room for Mark!"
- Or, she can choose to ignore the remark and remain in her seat.

THESE ARE the different types of "listening."

Active Listening

The essential skill for easy small talk and successful interactions with people is:

- Paying attention means hearing and understanding what's being said accurately.
- Reflection: You are then able to interact successfully.
- Respond: Offer concise feedback.

Selective Listening

This takes place when you are disinterested in the topic:

- Low attention span.
- Choose to remember only portions of the discussion.
- Uninterested in being part of the discussion.

Example: When someone starts talking about football with a group of ladies from the knitting club—a taboo subject you are not comfortable with—a topic that you find boring.

Empathic Listening

An introverted specialty makes you more endearing to people once they get to know you, for example:

- Picking up on emotional signals.

- Listening attentively, tuning into the other person's emotional state, and matching their mood but not evaluating.
- Reading between the lines and understanding the true meaning behind what's being said.

QUALITIES of a Good Listener

- Keep looking at the speaker and making eye contact.
- Don't look around distractedly while the other person is talking; focus.
- Don't be biased or prejudicial—listen without filters.
- Ask appropriate questions: why, how, when, and where.
- Summarize and give feedback confirming you were paying attention.

What Do I Gain From Becoming a Good Listener?

Listening will do more than improve your casual talking skills. You become more endearing to people and successful in other areas of your life.

Form Lasting Bonds With Friends

When you listen and offer constructive or sympathetic feedback, you show you care by paying attention. Most people are in desperate need of someone to listen to them, and having the patience to do so accurately will earn you positive friendships.

Promote Yourself as Curious and Intelligent

Actively listening shows you are attentive and curious; these are traits of an intelligent person who is thoughtful and caring. Plus, others will notice the quality in you.

Learn Speech From Others

Since we are naturally curious and learn through observation, listening is an excellent method for fine-tuning our speaking skills. Watching others talk will help you pick up on styles of presentation that are endearing to others and those that are not. If you are sketchy when it comes to giving a speech or talking in front of a group, listening to confident people explain themselves, cite their sources, and garner everyone's attention is an excellent way to learn by mirroring their actions.

Identify Your Listening Style and Those of Others

Since listening is a process that is conducted through our brains, we each develop a particular style of listening. You may connect with one of these types and also learn more about the types of listeners you meet.

Time-Oriented Listener

The impatient listener is basically on a timer. They cannot stay focused for long and do not appreciate long speeches. If the speaker potters about with details, they will lose focus; they will look around, turn away from the speaker, check their watch, and even look annoyed. Ultimately, they will tune out the speaker. When you identify such people and notice these traits, keep your speeches short and to the point.

The People-Oriented, Connective, and Emphatic Listener

A listener who tries to form a connection with the speaker is understanding and will place importance on the speaker and try to see every point from the other person's perspective while trying to learn more about the speaker than what they are saying. If you try to reflect the mood and thoughts of what the speaker is projecting and try to understand what they are saying from *their* point of view, you are a connected listener.

Cut to the Chase: The Action-Oriented Listener

This listener is not interested in fluff; tell them what you want them to do or know up front, or else they will lose interest. This listener is not interested in the story leading up to the chase; explanations and evidence are irrelevant—tell them what is needed and stop wasting their time.

Conceptual Forethought Listener

If you are modern and wide-ranging in your thinking, you like to go with the trends and will be open to harnessing future projections as part of your thought process. This type of listener works well within a group of people who are planning and conceptualizing future projects.

Analytical and Detailed Content Listener

You are interested in the content of what is being said. Facts, figures, and details are what get you interested in a conversation. The analytical listener has no patience for a "perhaps"—they need the points to be clear and verified. The only way a conversation will hold your interest is if you are satisfied with what's being said. You will keep asking questions—why, when, and how—and will only stop when you are satisfied. On a fun note: You are a tough cookie to please, and you are that one person in a group who will keep disrupting the self-promoter with diabolical questions.

Are Their Barriers to Listening?

Yes! It's called noise. And it can be any kind of, well, noise that prevents you from being heard or from hearing and comprehending what the speaker is saying.

- Physical noise: Loud chatter, someone's cell phone going off, etc., during a speech are simple physical noise barriers that can interrupt communication.
- Physiological noise: This one is hard to control as it concerns physiological barriers that block the flow of communication: The other person is tired, sick, hungry, unable to hear and see normally, and so on. While communicating, watch for signs of physiological noise and adjust how you communicate.
- Semantic noise: Barriers happen when the speaker's words are misinterpreted. Speaking in advanced

medical jargon is a fine example, such as when a doctor explains the procedures of a surgery to a layman.

- Psychological noise: Is based on personal characteristics. Attitudes and biases all fall into this category of the barrier. Understand that what they say will get filtered through personal assumptions, which become barriers at times.

Overcoming Assumptions, and Identifying Facts and Opinions

Assumptions can be the biggest barrier to initiating small talk. The following tips are based on generalized fears or assumptions that most people harbor when it comes to actively participating in a conversation.

- Stop assuming the worst—as an introvert who values your privacy, one of your biggest fears will be being asked too many questions and being perceived as "nosey." But that is your perception; get out of your mind; not everyone thinks in that context. Ask questions to show you are interested and get the other person talking.
- Be observant and identify a genuine interest in the other person. Once you see that they are truly interested in learning more about you and communicating with you, it will be easier to feel comfortable in the conversation and enjoy a good chat. You must radiate the same level of interest to put the other person at ease and create a firm bond.
- Assuming the worst—this means avoiding or going into a conversation with a preconceived negative notion of the other person. Such assumption barriers stop you from forming an honest opinion

based on experience and prevent you from enjoying what could be an interesting dialog.

How to Avoid the Negative Side Effects of Assumptions

Enjoy forming new relationships and getting to know people outside of your close-knit circle of friends, and also appear as an approachable and amicable person, by practicing the following techniques:

- Don't be closed-minded. Be open to new ideas, suggestions, and plans. Always assume there is something to learn from listening to the other person.
- Rely on your common sense and exchange biases for reasons. You will be surprised at how easy it is to talk to people when you treat every encounter as a new experience.
- Avoid being a stick in the mud, embrace change, and combine new encounters with past experiences.
- Go ahead and take notes. There is nothing wrong with some enthusiastic learning techniques.

More on Active Listening

Paying attention, reflecting, and responding to a conversation are the factors that govern active listening. It's a primary skill you will need to ace small talk based on both hearing and body language.

The "5-L" concept, used to teach toddlers the art of paying attention physically, is a fine example for us to adopt when striving to achieve active listening.

- Legs: Cross your legs or sit on the floor or in a chair with your feet grounded.

- Lap: Fold your hands in your lap.
- Listen: Prick up your ears and focus on what you're hearing.
- Lips: Shush and listen; do not interrupt.
- Look: Lock eyes with the speaker; show them you are listening and interested.

Fine Tuning Your Active Listening Skills

Active listening is not hard for an introvert to master; you are probably already a passive listener, sensitive to what's being discussed around you. Now learn how to turn that skill into a more positive encounter.

The Seven Fundamentals for Practicing Active Listening

Method	Why	How to Achieve	Sample
Question:	To build your data bank and know more about the speaker.	Keep asking questions with regard to the speaker or what they are talking about.	"So, you went back and complained, or did you walk away?"
Repeat or paraphrase:	Repeating yourself shows you are following the conversation. It's the motivation for the speaker to continue the dialog.	Repeat what you just heard by restating the information in your own words.	"Ah, so you finally found the address."
Mirror emotions and feelings:	Reflect empathy and understanding of the speaker's emotional state. Encourage them to share their feelings and emotions. Allow the speaker	Mirror the speaker's emotions and how they are feeling through words, tone, and body language. Ask questions that encourage sharing.	"You must have felt *so* sad!' "How did you feel afterwards?" "I totally get why it was exciting!'"

	to evaluate their emotional state.	Respond with the same enthusiasm.	
Interpret:	Clarify what you just heard to make sure you are both on the right track. Also, to help the speaker broaden their perspective.	Question hazy declarations. Repeat incorrect explanations and subtly encourage the speaker to reevaluate their claims.	"Let me get this right; you think the cause for the breakdown was the lack of *oil* in the engine?"
Motivate:	Encourage the speaker to keep going by showing interest. Put down distractions and give 100% attention.	Argue and offer alternate solutions or ideas. Make the conversation debatable. Use different tones of voice to elicit interest, doubt, and excitement. A nod to show agreement. Use phrases such as "aha," "hm," and "oh."	"Oh my, when the lady turned and came back angry at the mistake, were *you* still there?" "Well, that makes perfect sense." "How did it impact you?"
Balance:	Keep asking for more detail and, in the process, help the speaker analyze their feelings as well.	Question specific points and statements.	"What happened when you realized your student was to blame for the accident?"
Assess:	Review the conversation thus far. Summarize all you heard and make the connections to broaden the discussion.	Repeat the main points you heard, as well as summarize the emotions and feelings involved.	"I believe the main focus and stress, for you, were in this area..."

Here Are a Few Points to Keep in Mind to Be a Better Listener:

•   Stay focused as you listen. Don't interrupt, and don't distract yourself by thinking about what to say next. Listen to what's being said. Be open-minded and avoid judging until you have heard the full story.

- Watch out for nonverbal cues. How a person presents themselves shows in their tone of voice, actions, and general demeanor—excited, nervous, cautious, etc.

- Patience should be a virtue.

- Question and ask for clarifications when you don't understand.

- Return your attention to the conversation at hand. It's natural for your mind to wander. Consciously bring it back to the present conversation.

- Develop cognitive empathy—tune into the speaker's mind and feelings to form a link and a better understanding of the emotional state behind what's being said.

Let's swing back to casual conversations' main axis—confidence. You need the confidence to stay in control of a conversation, take over the reins, and lead a successful discussion.

But how do you build up the courage to *start* a conversation?

The next chapter is all about how to arm yourself with enough confidence to approach strangers and strike up a conversation with conviction.

5

GEARING UP YOUR CONFIDENCE

All those iconic presenters of today were a shy little kid back then. –
Aayush Jain

E dith sat in the corner of the dance hall and watched her kid learn to do a plié. Out of the corner of her eye, she shot a look at the group of parents, who were having a friendly chat. Edith's daughter was new to ballet class; she longed to join the group of parents as she had been sitting in the corner for two hours. She was reluctant to make the first move or engage in small talk.

"What if they ignore me? What do I talk about? They look as though they are old friends."

These thoughts filled her mind, but had she made eye contact with the others; she would have caught a friendly and inviting smile.

Edith spent most of her day in isolation; her husband worked long shifts, and she had no friends. Her duties as a wife and mom took up all her time, and she ached for human contact. But Edith lacked self-confidence.

Edith saw herself as boring, quiet, and with nothing interesting to talk about, which was not true. A lack of self-esteem can make you see yourself in an unfairly negative light. Let's dispel that notion.

Don't Let Doubt Silence You

No one expects you to be a master of ceremonies.

By being confident and accepting of yourself, you can avoid setting the bar too high. A relaxed and confident mind is more conversational.

Glossophobia, the fear of public speaking, is a common phobia linked to social phobia. Here are some statistics to prove you are not alone in dreading conversations in public (Zauderer, 2022):

- Over the age of 18, social phobias affect 40 million people.
- In the US, 75% of people are afraid of public speaking in some way.
- About 90% of people admit to being shy.

Introverts can become skilled public speakers because they like being slow and steady and are observant and sensitive, which are successful techniques for public speaking.

Public speaking includes official presentations and speeches, offering input at meetings, adding comments to a conversation, and being actively engaged with people at social events.

Gaining the confidence to speak up or talk to strangers is not something you are expected to learn in quick steps; it's a slow process that requires practice and building self-esteem along the way. To discover your voice, you must start by changing some of your characteristics and ideals.

Talk to Anyone: Build Your Confidence

Forget about your lack of skill in casual conversation. Stop stressing and focus on your inner needs.

What do you need to feel confident?—to be brave enough to walk up to someone and strike up a conversation.

You need to let go of self-doubt to get it out of your head and stop listening to the voices in there. Forget your fears about looking foolish, and stop selling yourself short. Then you can focus on what the other person is saying.

Techniques to FEEL Confident

The following techniques are designed to change the way you perceive your own abilities because, to be confident with strangers, you must first be confident with yourself.

Follow these rules:

Stop Looking for Validation From Others

It's important to keep in mind that the other person's response is not a reflection of yourself or your conversational abilities. We cannot control the reactions of others, which can be influenced by external factors such as stress, bad moods, family problems, etc. Avoid thinking too much about what the other person is thinking *about you*; they are probably busy thinking about *themselves* and their impact on you.

Follow Your Goals

Self-discipline rewards you with confidence. There is no greater boost to your ego than knowing you're on track to achieving your goals.

Goal setting must be done in moderation.

For example, let's say your ambition is to take part in a 5-mile sea swim. You cannot take part without training. Therefore, training, getting fitter, and building stamina are short-term goals you must achieve to reach your ultimate goal—the 5-mile swim.

Likewise, set small goals to help you overcome the fear of talking to strangers. Practice in small steps. Say "hello" to the neighbor you avoid in the hallway. Strike up a conversation with a person you're standing in line with, and so on. Be consistent, and record your progress if that helps.

Show Yourself Some Love

Want to be respected by others? Respect yourself! Don't be your own critic.

There is no greater elixir to uplift your soul and build self-confidence than a little TLC and respect thrown your way—it must come from you and no one else. Self-love is one of the greatest motivators out there because when you treat yourself with respect, you radiate the same sentiment, and others can pick up on that.

That little nagging voice in your head that keeps undermining your abilities can cause damage.

Turn negativity into positivity and override doubtful thoughts with motivational affirmations you can keep repeating when you feel nervous. Try these:

- I am in control.
- I am capable.
- I am not nervous; I'm awesome and special.

Visualize Success

The power of manifestation is too great to ignore; you can manifest success by visualizing.

Use the luxury of imagination to see yourself strutting confidently up to someone and striking up a very powerful and interesting conversation.

Nowhere in that visualization is there room for self-doubt; you have nailed casual talk, and there is no turning back—high five!

Practice visualization when you know you have a function to attend. Use a trusty old mirror for some motivational self-talk and envision your success.

Tap Into Your Limbic System

This part of your brain regulates feelings and behavior. An important function is initiating your fight-or-flight mode, which served men in prehistoric times by keeping them safe—a time when conversation was simple and limited.

I'm talking about going with your good old-fashioned gut feeling, also known as the limbic system, to give you accurate insights; chat up the friendly-looking person or ignore the grumpy boss.

You can also look at the person's eyes while talking; if they are staring intently at you while you talk, they are interested. If they keep looking over your shoulder or move their head around, they are bored or distracted. Feet are also a good indication, as people tend to point their feet in the direction of their interests. Someone standing with their feet and slightly away from you may not be fully immersed in the conversation.

Learn more about the fascinating language of body language and sharpen your skills for deciphering nonverbal communication by exploring Book 2, which delves deeper into deciphering automatic physical signals the other person sends. It's a comprehensive guide to decoding subtle, unconscious messages the other person is sending through actions, tone of voice, facial expressions, and other physical cues. Deciphering these cues will help you to fine-tune your conversation skills, gain a preview of the other person's emotional response, and become more conscious of *your* body language.

Practice Mindfulness

Mindfulness meditation is the art of enjoying the present moment. The practice makes you more focused, sharper, and observant. Mindfulness is ideal for stilling unwanted thoughts in your mind so you can concentrate on the present moment. It helps to actively listen to the talker, formulate clear replies, and become immersed in the conversation. So, when listening to someone talk about their trip to Thailand, your mind remains focused and not on the fried chicken you ate last night for dinner.

How to practice mindfulness:

Example: If enjoying an evening walk, begin with deep breaths. Focus on your walking. One step in front of the other. Look around and observe. If random thoughts enter your mind, don't let them linger. Become immersed in your act of walking and focus on only that. Practice makes perfect; use the techniques for almost any activity, even when washing the dishes.

Techniques to LOOK Confident
Stand Tall and Proud

I don't mean to puff your chest out and flex your muscles; instead, a good stance, square shoulders, and a head held high can radiate an aura of confidence. Just as you are conscious of the other person's body language, they are of yours. Slumped shoulders, eyes that keep darting all over the place, and a jittery stance show you are nervous or scared, and that changes how other people interact with you. Displaying honesty and looking confident will certainly attract a few interested people.

Quit Formulating Answers—Listen First

Despite feeling excited and wanting to rattle off some productive answers, don't keep making mental notes of good comebacks while the other person is speaking—you lose focus on the gist of the conversation. Listen intently, absorb, then reply. Otherwise, you sound rude and interruptive, like a kid who can't wait his turn to talk.

Example of what not to do:

- Other person: "Hi, nice to meet you. I'm the account manager at the agency."
- You (in your head): "Oh, she sounds important. I'm just the office clerk. Maybe I should avoid talking about my job; what can I say that sounds important..."

Talk to Impress

Your tone of voice and pace of speaking can evoke confidence, fear, or annoyance. Talk clearly, slowly, and loudly enough to be heard. Mumbling will earn you some stares, a polite nod of the head, and lots of goodbyes.

Your voice is representative of your character and self-confidence; use it to promote yourself and garner interest. You cannot change your voice to suddenly sound as smooth as velvet, but you can learn to control how you sound and use tone to animate what you are saying.

Try these tips:

- Don't trip over your words; slow down and talk in clear sentences. Don't speak slower than the person you are talking to; match their pace.
- Speak up in a strong voice that's audible for everyone to hear—turn a few heads.
- Take deep breaths, so you don't sound winded when you talk.
- Speak in full sentences; don't add lots of "ums" and "errs" to the conversation, and show them you know what you're talking about.
- Practice: Record a fake conversation and see how you sound. Mousey, nervous, too excited, creepy? Keep changing until you get an even, smooth, and audible tone.

Radiate Happiness

Check out a room full of people. How big is the circle around the bubbly, laughing person compared to the grumpy, disgruntled-looking guy suspiciously sniffing his drink?

Try to adopt a lighter take on life; laugh when you can, choose to be happy, and avoid overthinking or being too dramatic. Your happiness radiates through you and is a good magnet to draw people toward you. Besides, being easygoing helps you to be funny and interesting without the hassle of biases.

Be Conscious of Your Nervousness

Avoid trying to hide your nervousness. Be conscious of how you feel and work around the emotion. It's okay to feel nervous but do not let it silence you. Talk clearly and audibly, and as you hear the confidence in your voice, it will help gradually dispel your inhibitions.

Know When to Be Quiet

Eric was a nervous chatterbox; he would present his facts successfully but add some totally useless comments to fill the silence. It showcased him as nervous and made people reluctant to trust him or stay in conversation with him.

When you have just stood up for yourself or made a really good pitch, you should rather "shut up."

It's okay to avoid irrelevant chatter if you have successfully asserted yourself. Not being able to stand your ground and wait for a response makes you look insecure.

As an introvert, you may be comfortable going straight into facts—that's fine.

- Use humorous opening lines only if you are comfortable and experienced doing so—jokes that fall flat are not kind to your self-confidence.
- Wait for the other person to digest what they heard, formulate a reply, or even try staring you down if you just raised a dispute with them.
- No matter how nervous you feel about the awkward silence, wait for the reply.

Now that you have learned the talk, can you handle projecting your confidence through your physical self?

Your linguistic style, being more assertive and less affirmative, are skills that boost and project confidence—let's explore them.

———————————

Dear Reader,

For any author, positive customer reviews are the lifeblood of our livelihood. By leaving a friendly review of this book, you'll show other introverts where they can find the guidance to help them develop themselves and make a positive impact in their lives and the lives of others. On their behalf and mine, thank you for your support! You can snap the QR code below or visit Amazon here.

6

LOOKING AND SOUNDING CONFIDENT BECAUSE APPEARANCES MATTER

To be noticed without striving to be noticed—this is what elegance is about. –Luciano Barbera

This chapter is about images. We discuss how you project yourself through looks and talk. Also, did you know that confidence can be channeled through your tone of voice, your stance, and your demeanor?

Power Talk Works!

In the business world, power talk can make or break deals. Even the phrase "power talk" evokes images of smartly dressed men smoking cigars and talking about world dominance. While "world dominance" may stretch the depiction a bit, the image of *men* looking powerful is much closer to the truth.

In the US, it's common practice to favor individuals who project themselves confidently through dialog rather than those who look and sound less confident—although qualification levels between the two parties may be the same, looks and confidence seem to win out.

On this theory, women often get overlooked when it comes to impressing. I am not starting a gender bias here; we are merely looking at facts. Women, while being just as assertive, will downplay their capabilities, while men will try to cover up their weaknesses. It's modesty versus boastfulness.

A study of social media language proves this theory, where affiliation and assertiveness were compared. Women used affiliative language, although just as assertive, compared to their male counterparts, who favored aggressive, colder, and less personal language, which invariably highlighted them as more assertive (Park et al., 2016).

Confidence Over Boasting: Stereotypes Based on Sex

Your behavior verbally matters; men will project their strengths at levels that women would often consider boastful.

Confident women see no need to promote themselves; they will choose to be humble rather than project themselves as overly confident. The female instinct to be nurturing and sensitive to the needs of others is also an influential factor.

Linda and Jon were both up for a promotion—a special project at the company's new branch in Thailand. Both were equally qualified and interviewed by the CEO.

During the interview, Linda was cool and collected. She knew the CEO knew about her qualifications and levels of responsibility, so she saw no need to promote herself verbally —that would be boasting.

Jon, on the other hand, was equally confident and not ashamed to show it. He made a very impressive speech that was the deal-breaker. He looked and *sounded* confident enough that the CEO saw him as the best person for the job.

A study conducted on gender-based self-declarations of academic results proved the theory that women downplay their abilities while men tend to be overly confident (Daubman et al., 1992). Gender stereotypes seem to be the influence here, where females are influenced by their nurturing nature and men by their primal need to be the alpha male. Although I must state that there are many assertive females who have successfully nailed gender stereotypes to be leaders in the business world, proving that anyone can improve their linguistic styles to become more confident—especially introverts, who are naturally more assertive, precise, and less abstract than extroverts.

Linguistic Style: The Next Level of Impressive Small Talk
How you say it and what you have to say matter!

Pair a very expensive-looking outfit with an accomplished linguistic style, and voila, you've got a formula for success.

We have thus far learned about the ins and outs of small talk, but now it's time to learn about projecting confidence linguistically.

Linguistic style is similar to carefully selecting an outfit that showcases your personality. Word choice, being subtle or direct, the use of metaphors and jokes, questions and stories, being apologetic when it helps, and promoting your good qualities, minus arrogance, is how to project a successful linguistic style.

Linguistic Patterns That Are Perceived as Negative
Avoid this style of talking.

- Waiting too long to reply during a pause means that you miss your turn to speak up, and bam, you get perceived as not having much to say or as someone with little confidence or interest in the discussion.

Another person: "I don't think you guys organized the party too well." (Here's your cue to jump in and debunk the statement, but you wait too long to reply.)

Another person: "Oh, well, maybe next time you can do better." (It's too late to reply now without opening an argument.)

- Being too direct—when subtlety is not practiced, others think you are rude, uncaring, or not a team player.

"I don't like those proposals; you need to change them." (This proposal is good; maybe we can fine-tune it a bit more.)

- Speaking much slower than the rest of the group is perceived as slow-thinking or unenthusiastic (even boring).

"So, er... I was at the... party, um, when we all went into... the garden..."

- Using low-confidence words such as "only," "maybe," "think," etc., deflates trust in what you say.

"This new engine oil is guaranteed, I think, to improve your car's performance."

Positive Linguistic Style

- Compliments: Remember, some people offer compliments as an automatic response, a ritual. Don't be hasty to go into critique mode unless you're sure it's been asked for. Vice versa, you must be prepared to receive criticism as a follow-up to a compliment.

Allison: "That was a very good speech, Collin. Well done."
Collin: "Thanks, Allison!"
Allison: "How was my presentation?"
Collin: "Well, there were several areas that could have been fine-tuned, such as..."

- Feedback: Be subtle with negative feedback.

"The table decor looks very pretty, Jean, thank you. Could we also add a few extra details...?"

Asking Questions: How and When Matters for Successful Linguistic Styles

Asking questions is the best way to exchange information and is often a conversation filler, but asking too many questions can make you look bad. For example:

- The one person in a group who asks more questions than the others is perceived as being less knowledgeable.
- Others think you are disinterested and not following the conversation, or you are slow to comprehend.
- You are perceived as high-maintenance.
- Asking too many questions at interviews makes employers think you will spend a lot of your time questioning rather than being proactive.
- Men see asking questions as a negative self-image (losing face). Hence their reluctance to ask for directions.

Therefore:

- Question only when necessary.
- File some questions for clarification in private.
- Follow the norm; if no one in the group is questioning, do the same.
- Follow the lead; if the conversation becomes a Q&A session, throw in a few that make others question the speaker's points as well.

Example: "At the risk of sounding ignorant, I may be the

only person here who doesn't understand why the water is poured through a funnel..."

- Questions that lead to apologies—get them right.

Example

- "Hi, Jace. Did the client like your presentation?"
- "No! Not really. They want me to redo the entire concept."
- "Oh, dear! I'm sorry. I know how much research you put into your presentation."

The Difference Between Arrogance and Confidence

A confident introvert dislikes showing off and is rarely arrogant. Based on the gender-stereotypical comparisons we made, being strongly assertive through language and character is essential. How, then, do you draw the line between assertiveness and being arrogant?

How do Arrogant People Behave?

Mostly seeking fame, they love being in the spotlight.

- They enjoy talking about themselves.
- Belittle others and are condescending.
- They will openly act bored when the talk is not centered on them and display body language to match.
- They dread looking bad and are reluctant to admit a mistake.

An arrogant person will see themselves as confident and hope to project the same. However, being boastful and arrogant is often interpreted by others as being insecure and needing validation. This is a put-off for most people who tend to beat a hasty retreat, and I make a mental note to avoid such people in the future.

What Is Confidence?

It's feeling self-assured. A confident person does not need to validate themselves unless the need calls for it, for example:

- They are self-assured, know what they know, and see no need to broadcast their achievements, etc.
- When needed, they will assert their capabilities without stepping on others.
- They do not seek glory; they are helpful and seek help.
- They are happy to validate others, are good listeners, and are open to learning new things.

While fellowship and affiliations are important, a healthy dose of confidence will not go unnoticed. Find a balance to remain comfortable talking about your achievements and abilities. It's needed for forming vital connections, personal growth, and looking confident to others, which, in turn, will pique their interest in you, leading to easier, immersive, and lengthy conversations.

Taking Care of Your Appearance and Why Does It Matter?

"If you only saw the look on her face!"

How many times have you heard that or repeated the statement yourself?

Facial expressions can create an impression and are almost always the first point of physical contact.

Facial cues reveal more than you think. Book 2 elaborates more on the point, but for now, it suffices to say that your facial expressions overgeneralize certain traits and characteristics about you—specific emotions like anger or annoyance; babyface, which showcases a look of innocence; ill health; and the familiar face recognition hypothesis, where our eyes light up, or your expression softens when confronted by familiar people.

Therefore, facial expressions play a major role when it comes to small talk—encouraging people to approach you, warm to you, and believe what you say is genuine. A friendly, laidback smile will make it easier to break the ice than an apprehensive look of uncertainty because people radiate positivity.

How to Physically Generate Confidence

It takes practice to walk into a room full of strangers and look confident and positive, even if you are a quivering pot of Jell-O inside. But it is doable, and here are my tried-and-tested techniques.

The Power Pose

Here's where you trick your brain into believing you are confident. Open poses or power poses can do just that. Open up your body, expand, and take up more space as opposed to slouching, slumping your shoulders, and aiming to occupy as little space in the universe as possible.

- Strike a pose. Before you go into a room full of people or a presentation, strike an open pose— hands up in the air and feet apart. Do so discreetly just before your big debut and tell your brain, *I'm the boss, and I got this.*
- Stand with your feet apart, shoulders squared, and your head held high. Don't look arrogant; simply don't look scared, shy, or introverted.

Hand Cues

Use your hands to show openness. Open palms pointing outward are a good indication of confidence—especially during a presentation. Use strong hand gestures to show respect, open-ness, and acceptance.

- Raised hand signals, palms out, are an invitation to open a dialog; don't point, as it can be perceived as arrogance.
- Lay your hands out on the table and hunch forward as an indication of interest in what the other person is saying.
- Never fold them up against your chest—it depicts a barrier and looks aggressive, as though you disagree with what's being said.

Make Eye Contact

- Look them in the eye.

Compose Facial Features
Control your facial cues with the following example:

- Don't squint or furrow your brows unless you are trying to match the other person's emotion.
- Listen to the dialog with a smile (not if it's sad news).
- Avoid projecting a negative or aggressive image, which can happen unintentionally if you don't pay attention to your facial expressions—such as squinting from sunlight, thinking about your noisy neighbor while engaging in a chat, and so on.

Looking Confident and Dressing to Impress
Practice self-care to look and feel confident externally and internally. The latter will certainly influence your aura and can be achieved by sticking to the following emotional self-care goals:

- Nurture your body—eat a healthy and balanced diet. Sticking to a wholesome eating pattern will enhance your body and mind. Become more alert, think clearer, and improve your attention span.
- Exercise: If you dread the word "exercise," exchange it for physical activity—anything that you enjoy: swimming, dancing, walks, jogging, yoga, gardening, and so on. It's good for your cognitive health, offers emotional balance, and helps you to remain alert.
- Maintain close friendships and spend time with them. Make connections with the community you live in; a good start to making small talk is chatting with people in your neighborhood.
- Relax and unwind; meditate, do yoga, take long walks, get massages, and sometimes even a nice long soak in the tub can work wonders.

Dressing to Look Confident

You don't need designer suits to dress impressively. Look smart and confident, whether you are a CEO or a student, by following these tips.

Follow these tips to avoid feeling awkward and wishing you hadn't worn what you did:

- Choose clothes that feel like your second skin. When you dress to feel comfortable, your mind is relaxed, and conversation is easier when you're not thinking about how your stomach bulges because the pants are too tight, for example. Also, you can practice open poses and not use your arms to cover any body parts.
- Avoid following new trends that make you uncomfortable, such as wearing four-inch heels when you prefer sneakers.

- Wear dark colors for meetings; they spell confidence. Black, for example, is authoritative, while red is aggressive and dominant but also elegant and friendly.
- Follow dress codes: Do not show up for a black-tie event in sneakers and jeans. You will feel out of place and insecure. Unless, of course, that is your signature style, and you can confidently rock the outfit.
- Dress to impress yourself and not to conform to modern trends.

Have a Positive Conversation With Yourself

Influence your subconscious mind with positive self-talk.

This technique is ideal for getting in tune with your thoughts, emotions, ideals, and questions. You can use self-talk positively or negatively.

Be pessimistic with your thoughts and condition your mind toward a forward-thinking outlook, which has several benefits, including better health, a cheerful outlook, and less anxiety. The theory has been researched, with studies proving the point (Conversano et al., 2010).

Here Are Some Positive Self-Talk Phrases to Use

- What I did took courage, and I am proud of myself.
- It's my right to change my mind. Other people will understand.
- I am going to become stronger and healthier.
- I will recover my health and do it for myself.
- I am important, and I must take care of myself.
- I have the power to make this work because I am strong and capable.

Feel free to add more phrases as you feel appropriate. By

improving your self-talk, you are building confidence to talk to other people. Self-talk is managed by your critical inner voice, the one that says, "I can" or "I can't."

How to Use Self-Talk to Soothe and Learn to Talk to People

1. Use pronouns to have conversations with yourself.

Let's say you are considering approaching a circle of people you have never met. What kind of conversation will go on in your head?

Negative self-talk: "This is so embarrassing for me, standing here looking like a wallflower. What if I approach those people, and they are not friendly?"

What if you switched the above? Change the "I" statements to pronouns or the use of your name.

Positive self-talk: "Why are you standing here feeling embarrassed? Come on, Ross, do you really want to look like a loser? Try talking to them, man, and see if they are friendly."

Try this switch the next time you are debating with your mind and have a tough decision to make.

1. Use motivational self-talk.

Steer the conversation in your head toward a beneficial direction—it's your conversation, and you're the director.

Use motivational phrases that work for you.

"Come on, let's get this done!" or "You can do this!"

1. Avoid saying: "I can't."

"Can't" is a very negative phrase. Using "I don't" instead gives you control over your thoughts and the situation.

- "I can't walk into that room full of people." This sounds as though you have no control over the situation.
- "I don't want to look awkward walking into a crowded room." This sounds as though you have a choice.
- Therefore, you can go on to think, *Maybe it won't feel so awkward.*

1. Be your best friend.

Be the friend who gives yourself a pep talk when it's needed. Avoid demeaning yourself and thinking negatively.

Instead, *I will never get this right...* Rather think *I can nail this*!

1. Avoid rumination.

This means putting an end to constant worry. Social anxiety often gives way to rumination. Studies show that rumination is higher post-event—for example, you go home after a social event and berate yourself for not talking more (Perini et al., 2006).

Be conscious of this negativity and avoid ruminating. Use positive self-talk to tell yourself that you can do better next time. Or, better yet, use it plus open poses to nail the conversation, leaving no room for worrying post-event.

1. Criticize your criticism.

Every time you entertain a critical thought, you are lowering your confidence. Avoid this by beginning to question your criticism of yourself.

"I suck at making small talk!"

"Do I really suck? I'm not that bad. I can manage a few jokes and make some interesting remarks when I want to!"

Mirror Work: Smile Through the Clouds

Smile in the mirror. Do that every morning, and you'll start to see a big difference in your life. –Yoko Ono

How easy is it to stay mad at someone who is smiling?

I find it quite impossible, and I know a few people who are suckers for their kids' cheeky smiles, no matter the grades or the fact they just recolored their living room walls with crayons.

The theory of smiling in the mirror can work for you in just the same way through mirror work. The technique, which involves looking at yourself in the mirror and repeating self-care affirmations, can help improve your self-worth, and you get to practice talking to yourself.

What are the benefits?

- Improve your communication skills.
- Become more positive and comfortable with how you look.
- It's motivational and boosts self-confidence.
- You become more accustomed to looking people in the eyes.
- You look more confident to other people.
- Put your doubts to rest.

Need I say more?

Mirror Techniques for Building Confidence

Check out these mirror work techniques that will help you stop being hard on yourself and get in touch with your true self.

Start your day smiling in the mirror and give yourself a physical boost because smiling is positive body language that tells your brain, "Hey, I'm confident, and I'm awesome."

- Reply to your beaming image by repeating a positive self-talk affirmation.
- Make a positive statement about the day:
- Today is going to be one of my best days!
- It's a beautiful day, and I am going to make the most of it!
- I expect only the best for me today.
- Repeat a confidence-building affirmation:
- I am proud of my abilities.
- I am interesting to talk to, and I can hold a conversation.
- I can connect with people.
- I am not nervous to speak up in a group.

Mirror work must be practiced twice a day, and through diligence, you can start to see results in two weeks. As you face your fears and inhibitions, learn more about your facial expressions and how to talk to people better.

Now that you have learned to read yourself, it's time to learn to read the other person. Reading body language can be quite insightful. Learn to read between the lines and pick up on what goes unsaid in casual conversations.

7

READING THEM LIKE AN OPEN BOOK

The human body is the best picture of the human soul. –Ludwig Wittgenstein

D o you often wish you could read minds so you knew what to say and who to approach? Much of your fear or anxiety over small talk is based on the unknown because if only you knew what to say and how to gauge the other person's thinking, you would not be so nervous second-guessing your impact on people. Well, reading body language can offer you that, and when practiced and learned with commitment, you can use the skill for your benefit because, after all, over half of our communication is done via nonverbal communication, aka body language.

Body Language to the Rescue

"Oh, boy, I'm glad they announced that Roger got the promotion. I was dreading the appointment as it meant more work, and I really was not interested in the post."

Saying the above, Sara smiled at Kaeden, her boyfriend,

and reassured him that she was not upset about being passed up for the promotion. As she did so, Kaeden noticed her blink several times and avoided looking him in the eye.

On these cues, Kaeden knew Sara was really extremely upset and was trying her best to hide her disappointment; therefore, he was able to be subtly sympathetic and distract her by taking her out to the movies and showering her with care.

This is merely an example of how useful reading body language can be.

The 7/38/55 Formula: How Important Is Reading Body Language?

A person's body language can be read to successfully decipher what's not being said, thus helping you to improve on the conversation, steer clear of what seems to be taboo subjects and be more intuitive to what's going on with the other person.

As the 7/38/55 formula theory proves, body language makes up a larger portion of communication, and reading it is kind of like having a magic-looking glass into the other person's emotions and thoughts (Park & Park, 2018b).

Plus, you become more emotionally aware, manage to establish trust with others easily, bond with coworkers, successfully make your point understood, and impress while influencing. You go from relying on perception to reality.

For example, the moment the other person crosses their arms or taps their feet, you know it's time to change the subject, pose your face, and continue with a positive conversation.

Likewise, you can avoid projecting the wrong body language yourself, which can happen unintentionally at times. Besides, once you learn body language cues, you become more in control of what you reveal to the other person—a factor that appeals to the reserved nature of your introversion.

Negative Body Language to Avoid

"I was homesick and couldn't make it to your party, sorry."

Helen told Peter while looking at her work desk, hoping to

see the file she had requested sitting there. However, Peter took Helen's looking away as a sign of insincerity and her statement as a lie, although it was the truth.

You can unconsciously communicate nonverbally through the wrong body language, which can undermine or contradict what you are saying, for example:

- Slumping: It zaps your energy. You look less confident, disinterested in what's going on, and even worried and defeated.
- Crossed arms: This means you have gone on the defensive and have closed your mind off to what the speaker is saying.
- Avoiding direct eye contact: Distracted, disinterested, or avoiding being truthful.
- Face:
- Frowning denotes confusion, anger, and frustration.
- Flaring nostrils indicate disapproval, feeling defensive, or judgment is taking place.
- Fidgeting: This can be playing with an object at hand, such as twirling a pen, tapping feet, crossing or moving leg positions, etc., which can indicate disinterest, boredom, or being under stress.
- Leaning back: This is an "I don't care" gesture. Or, "This is not a serious situation. Let's move on" kind of vibe you're sending.
- Using hands to chop air: You know this gesture; it comes out when people are excited about what they are saying. It's an annoying gesture for others who see it being virtually axed out of the picture.
- Touch your nose or face, and it's an indication of deception or defiance, especially if you listen silently while touching your face.

- Head nodding: If you do this a lot during a conversation, it makes you look weak or like you don't really care either way because you are nodding in agreement to every word.
- Don't touch someone with your fingertips; it says, "Ew, I can barely touch you." Touch is a great way to form a bond. Try a pat on the back, etc.

Learning to Read Body Language Successfully

Before we begin, let's address the elephant in the room glaring back at us: Can body language be faked?

To a certain extent, yes!

But our nonverbal reactions are automatic and connected to our emotions, and unless you are perfectly in tune with and in charge of emotional regulation, it's hard to avoid auto-reflexes.

You can control your body language to a certain degree by controlling the actions we discussed earlier under negative body language.

For example: Despite feeling defensive about what someone is saying, you can aim for a more amicable discussion instead of crossing your arms and tapping your foot, thus making them hostile toward you. You can listen and then propose your point of view.

While you can understand the dynamics of body language in its entirety in my second book, here's how to read body language in a more analytical manner.

Look at Overall Signals and Inconsistencies

Just because someone looks away once while pledging undying affection to you, don't take it as an indication of infidelity—you've got to observe more.

Take in the overall behavior and body language of the person you are talking to. Consider the signals in a group, for example:

- eye contact
- hand movements
- posture
- tone of voice
- and inconsistent actions with what's being said, such as shaking the head in a "no" gesture while saying "yes." Do the actions match the words?

Go With Your Gut Feeling

Your limbic system is sharp and will pick up on inconsistencies between actions and words. If you have a gut feeling something is wrong, there is probably a mismatch between what you are hearing and seeing.

Pay Attention to Nonverbal Cues

- Are they making eye contact? Is it normal? Is it too intense and making you feel uncomfortable? They are probably trying their best to manipulate their nonverbal signals.
- The tone of voice: Is it warm, friendly, and laid-back, or high-pitched and strained? Someone smiling and talking in a high voice may be trying to hide stress.
- Body posture: Shoulders can be relaxed, hunched, or tense. Is their posture relaxed, or do they appear stiff and uncomfortable?
- Face: Is the face animated, depicting emotions that match what they are saying? Or is it guarded and expressionless?
- Touch. How creepy is the touch? Is it inappropriate? Or are you relaxed and comfortable enough to receive a friendly pat or touch on the arm? Use your intuition for this one. But do make sure before you go running off screaming sexual harassment that some people are naturally very "touchy."

- How engaged is the other person? What's their level of involvement in the conversation? Are they overly involved and listening intently, or disinterested and bored-looking?
- The response sounds like this: Do you hear any that means caring, concern, or stronger emotions like anger in relation to what you're saying? Such as sucking in breath loudly, clicking the tongue, whistling "wow," etc.
- The timing of nonverbal expressions is important. Do the facial and body cues come on too fast? Are they too intense? Do they seem fake? Or, is there a natural rhythm to how they display nonverbal signals?
- Holding their hands: The clasped hand is a classical sign of self-doubt or nervousness. The person is holding their own hand for comfort. Someone who wraps their legs around the legs of furniture is sending similar signals.
- Placing hands in pockets or clasping them behind their back means the person has a secret—something to hide.
- Touching the legs and patting them. This indicates insecurity, and the patting is a gesture of self-soothing.

The Resting Bitch Face

The resting bitch face (RBF) is responsible for people sometimes asking you if you had a bad day or why you are angry. Perhaps you've seen random photos of yourself looking as though you were the moodiest person on Earth at events where you thought you were smiling and looking happy.

Women are more susceptible to the RBF, except for a few

men. A fine example of a male with an RBF is Kanye West. (Aha, do you get what expression I am talking about now?) Having this expression does not mean you are in a bad mood; you could be feeling neutral while your face is displaying the emotions of a permanently upset person. A slightly down-turned and angled mouth that makes you look smug and like a "depressed bulldog."

While dealing with an RBF should not be a major issue, it can be a put-off for most people who perceive you as contemptuous and unapproachable.

So, there you are at the party, a glass of gin in hand, happily surveying the crowd and thinking of some witty small-talk anecdotes. But alas, unknown to you, you've got your bitch face on. And while you feel friendly and approachable inside, your face is telling people to back off and leave you alone.

Proving the theory of the RBF by evoking images of negative emotions is done through tests with face-reading software designed to pick up emotions. On a totally negative face, the software will register close to 97% negativity and 3% emotions (Gibson, 2016). On an RBF, the software picks up 6% of emotions, double the normal percentage, and showcases underlying emotions in those people. The reason for developing an RBF is not established, with some scientists claiming it is partially due to natural features.

Celebrities Who Can't Help Looking Frumpy

These celebrities, despite being in the limelight, must deal with their RBF.

Kristen Stewart

The actress has been called out several times for her unsmiling bitch face and has gone on to state she does smile a lot, except the cameras don't seem to capture much of it.

Queen Elizabeth

The late queen was a champion for maintaining composure, and despite being strict about showing any type of emotion, the monarch could not escape the dreaded RBF and often appeared looking like a strict schoolmarm.

Get Rid of Your Resting Bitch Face to Look More Approachable:

- Smile: Use a smile to transform your angled mouth from a grimace into one of happiness.
- Turn your eyes up, tilt your head back, and look up at people. The action will open up your eyes more, and you'll avoid the slanted slits of an RBF.
- Tongue in teeth: Touch your tongue to the back of your front teeth. The action helps you smile more and relaxes your facial muscles.
- Rock your RBF: If you can't beat it, own it. Accept what nature has bestowed on you, and don't rely on your face to garner friendships or strike up a conversation. People can be impressed through intuitive talk and positive actions.

On the subject of impressing people, the next chapter deals with improving your speech to charm and influence others into forming bonds with you. Let me help you understand the importance of tone, words, and choice of topic to keep a good conversation flowing.

8

FINE TONING YOUR SPEECH TO IMPRESS

Sometimes, the people you think don't want to talk to you are the ones waiting for you to talk to them. –Unknown

Voice tone is essential for sending across the right message.

Jason was the headmaster at his local high school, but assembly day, where he would attempt to interact with his students by making jokes and talking about important life lessons, always fell flat. The kids would look bored, fidget, and slump in their chairs. Jason noticed all this from his spot on the stage and felt disappointed at his students' lack of interest.

However, if Jason had stepped back and sat in the audience to listen to himself, he would have dozed off in the first five minutes.

As interesting as his stories were, no matter how funny his jokes were, the tone of his monotonous, drone-like, and lackluster voice was sad. There were no highs and lows to animate what he was saying. No excitement punctuated the air; everything was one long drawl, and no one cared to listen to him.

Exploring Tonality

Speak in such a way that others love to listen to you. Listen in such a way that others love to speak to you. –Anonymous

Anyone who loves listening to Barack Obama speak will understand the meaning of the above quote. The former president is laidback yet assertive and speaks in friendly, inviting tones that help him deliver his messages clearly and with the full attention of his audience. Obama is a "motivator," someone who possesses the skill to talk in tones that ignite interest in others.

What Are the Four Types of Tone?

1. Educator—the informative tone (the type of tone Jason, our headmaster, should use).
2. Motivator—creates inspiration.
3. Colleague—friendly tone, informal, and conversational tone.
4. Coach—the assertive voice that gives direct instructions.

How Important Is Tone of Voice?

Tonality refers to the tone your voice takes when you speak to people. The right tone will help you get your message across successfully; the wrong tone will make people reject what you say or even shut you off.

It's important to gauge your audience and the message you are delivering when choosing a tone of voice. Tone can be used like body language to convey "nonverbal" messages and let others know your feelings—how passionate, sad, angry, or excited you are feeling.

Here are some examples to prove tone is important:

- Did you know that the "Iron Lady," the late Margret Thatcher, considered tone so important that she used the services of a professional vocal coach to help her raise the cadence of her voice to sound more authoritative? She learned to control her tone and lower or raise the volume of her voice to deliver successful speeches and maintain her tough leadership persona.
- Men with a richer voice pitch are paid more, according to studies (Grant, n.d.). Certainly, an incentive to improve your tone.
- Doctors are meant to use a soft, informative, and caring tone of voice. Some who do not are linked to malpractice accusations (Ambady et al., 2002).

How Do I Decide on My Tonality?

When we speak, we don't hear our voice in the same tone that others hear. We hear a deeper version where higher pitches are toned down. Air conduction and your skull are responsible for the alteration.

To hear an accurate tone of your voice, record yourself reading a script that includes animated reading, questions, and answers to identify tone and pitch for better control. A recorded version of your voice is the most accurate.

Listen for the following:

- Speed: More than 120 and less than 180 words per minute.
- Concentrate on words important to you in the conversation. How defined are they?
- Volume: Are you soft-spoken? Do people lean in to hear you speak? Experiment with different levels of your voice through the recording.

- Eloquence: How good are your pronunciations? Are you fluent in your speech, or is it punctuated with too many "errs" and "ums"? Practice until you're articulate when forming sentences.

Imagine a Powerful Voice for Yourself

Margret Thatcher went in for voice coaching, although, contrary to popular belief, she didn't need to train her voice to exude power because the Iron Lady was already a powerful figure and, therefore, naturally commanded a voice of power.

This theory, when tested, proved individuals in high-rank positions had an even pitch and fluctuating volumes, which created a bigger impact, while those in lower-rank positions had pitch variations and softer volumes, projecting a weaker image (Ko et al., 2014).

Here's where open poses (arms out), practicing powerful self-talk phrases, and thinking positively help. You can condition your mind into a position of power and reap the benefits through the energized projection of your voice—the voice of power that says, "Hey, listen to me."

Speech Delivery

Presenting your facts to an audience is defined as "speech delivery." Speeches are often prepared dialogues that have been practiced. Yet there is nothing to stop you from getting the jitters every time you have to deliver a speech.

How Important Is Delivery?

The success of your speech delivery relies on verbal and nonverbal communication. The level of confidence you project verbally and nonverbally will determine how engaged your audience is since they will pick up on those cues to judge the credibility of your statements and whether you have researched the subject well. Therefore, use fluent statements with no "errs" and project a strong voice with an even tone.

Factors That Define the Effectiveness of a Speech

Pay attention to these factors to deliver an effective speech. Seeing an audience that's engaged and interested in what you are saying is a huge motivational factor for building confidence and encouraging you to continue with your talk.

- Choose an appropriate tone: Vary your tonality to suit the occasion. The type of voice you use to deliver a eulogy will not work at the opening ceremony of a fun arcade.
- Practice and prepare: Unpracticed speeches are disrupted with "errs" and "ums" and soon lose momentum as well as direction.
- Practice in front of a mirror.
- Research and know your facts.
- Focus on friendly and engaged faces in the audience and talk to them.
- Practice relaxing techniques before. Deep breathing, open poses, motivational self-talk phrases.
- Talk yourself into delivering an epic speech. "You got this, man; now, go out there and wow that audience!"
- Be confident.
- Depending on your topic, show empathy and practice emotional displays. Talking about defeating world hunger needs a sympathetic yet powerful projection of facial features and empathy in tone.
- Choose a fitting style: Deliver your speech in a style that fits the audience. You cannot speak to primary school kids about dinosaurs in the same language you would use with students studying for a degree in paleontology.

Concentrate on the following:

- Clarity
- Appropriateness
- Language simplicity

The preparation of supporting material and making sure any backup technology you are using is functioning will keep you focused and confident of a smooth delivery.

The Power of Figurative Speech

If you find explanations tough, using visual language or figurative speech to clarify what you are trying to explain is a good method.

Using Metaphors in Speech

A metaphor is an imaginative aid you use to explain a word, phrase, or sentence. Think of it as talking with an example already thrown in—figurative language.

"I've got to get home early; I have an early morning interview, and if I snooze, I lose."

No further explanation is needed once the above metaphor is added to the sentence. Metaphors make hard-to-explain ideas and theories more accessible as they create an illusion of what you are trying to convey. Therefore, using a metaphor in your speech when you find getting an idea across difficult is a good method to help your audience stay connected to what you are saying.

When using metaphors, use the following:

- They must be clear.
- Memorable
- Understandable
- Adaptable

Using Similes in Speech

Similes are not as powerful as metaphors; instead, they form a connection through a likeness to what you are trying to convey.

"I crashed the car because the fog was so thick, and I was as blind as a bat."

Words such as "are" or "like" can be added to enhance the meaning of sentences with similes. They are not as direct as metaphors and do not immediately create a mental image of what you are saying. But similes can be used to add an element of fun to your speech.

"I was so nervous on my date; I kept forgetting details as though my mind was like a blackboard that was erased."

Analogies That Clarify Speech

Use analogies when you need to compare one point with another. They are slightly more complicated than a metaphor but can be more clarifying.

"My experiences working in Greece were like helping myself to a jar of jelly beans blindfolded—I didn't know which flavor I was going to enjoy because the experiences were so varied and new to me."

Changing Your Tone: When, Where, and With Whom

The tone of your voice depends on the type of conversation you are having. There are four types:

1. **Discourse:** An amicable one-way conversation that successfully delivers information.

Example: A flight attendant explains safety protocols at takeoff.

2. **Debate:** An argumentative two-way discourse in which each speaker seeks to triumph.

Example: Two people arguing over which team will come

out on top at the next NFL

3. Dialogue: A pleasant conversation between two people.

Example: two friends talking about college days over coffee.

4. Diatribe: Anyone who uses manipulation, ultimatums, and dramatics to conduct a one-way conversation that's biased in their favor has a diatribe.

Example: a shopper trying to return an electrical item they used but no longer need.

Identify the type of conversation you are having and match the tone and rhythm.

Gender Differences When Communicating

It's fascinating to note that men and women conduct conversations differently. Starting from groups of giggling teenage girls to boys who look confused and nonplussed, gender communication differences do exist.

Gender Differences in Communication Styles

Males	Females
Are you blunt and very direct?	Emphasis on equality?
Like to tease and use slang as a way to bond?	Are you empathic and caring?
Are you worried about being emotional?	Are you emotional?
Are you brash and favor power debates?	Weaker in asserting themselves?
Are you very assertive and ambitious?	Are you less pushy?
Do you see collective decisions as a weakness?	Try to include a collective opinion when making a decision.
Are you more guarded with unsolicited feedback?	Offer feedback freely?
Do you use self-emphasizing plans?	Freely share information?
Are you guarded against asking too many questions?	Will you ask questions freely and be quick to apologize?

9

BUILDING RAPPORT AND MAINTAINING LINKS THROUGH COMMUNICATION

The greatest compliment that was ever paid me was when one asked me what I thought, and attended to my answer. –Henry David Thoreau

Making friends, impressing people, and enjoying socializing!

You are finally ready to step through the portal with enough tips, techniques, and confidence to master the art of casual conversation!

This chapter is your final boost. We are going to explore skills and techniques that will help you build rapport with strangers, find common ground to start a conversation, and make friendships.

Learn about breaking into a conversation circle, knowing what to say—and when not to say it—as well as strategies to impress and make a mark. By the end of this chapter, you will be armed with advanced conversation skills that will boost your levels of confidence and have you feeling more enthusiastic about social engagements as well as interactions with people you have never met.

Level Up Your Communication Game

Making small talk is not as easy as walking up to someone and chatting them up as though you are old friends. Well, not for most introverts, who struggle to come up with what to say and what to ask. But what if you had a set of rules to follow? A step-by-step guide to initiating and getting a conversation flowing.

Let me introduce you to the LOC method.

Listen—Observe—Compliment (LOC Method)

Use these three steps to build a conversation.

Listen

The first step is to be a good listener, as we have explored in Chapter 3, "Be a Good Listener." The importance of listening is highlighted throughout Chapters 1 and 2. Therefore, you know why this vital component of a casual talk is the initial step to coming up with good content to conduct a conversation.

Listen and collect your data, so you have enough in store to question and even use subtlety to ignite a passionate answer in the other person.

For example, if you are in a group conversation and listening to someone talk about people jumping the line at supermarkets. You can be crafty and wait for an opening in the conversation to recite an anecdote about how you were cut off by a rude customer who jumped the line at the bank. You know through observance that a statement is going to spark a reply from the other person, which can help the dialog move along.

Observe

Paying attention to people, their dress, talk, and actions is an ideal way to gather information for building a conversation.

For example: "I love those shoes. Are they real leather? Where did you get them from?" Or, "I couldn't help over-hearing your work at the Egyptian artifact department at the museum. I have been following the recent displays on ancient

Egyptian art and would love to have a discussion about their origins."

Compliment

Most people love others paying attention to them (even if it's not *your* style); therefore, a compliment can be a plus sign for the other person to take an interest in you and want to open up and have a conversation.

"Your speech was very insightful, and I learned a lot from the discussion."

"I heard you are responsible for organizing the charity drive. That must have been a lot of work. Well done. How did you manage?"

Acquaintance to Lifelong Friend—How to Make the Transition

Some people we meet for the first time make us feel at ease, and we sort of "clique" together. But then you end up going your separate ways and wondering what-if. Plus, it takes work to turn a casual acquaintance into a lifelong friend. But it is possible—even if you live miles apart.

Tips for Making Lifelong Friends

1. Get to know the person

Questions are gateways to great friendships and getting to know more about a person you meet for the first time. In Chapter 2, we explored the rules for asking engaging questions. Follow those guidelines and make sure to ask open-ended questions, leaving no room for one- or two-syllable answers.

"Hey there, how do you like working for the agency?"

1. Show your interest

Do not ask the person about their job, and keep looking over your shoulder. If you genuinely want to get to know them, become immersed in the conversation, show interest, ask run-on questions, and listen intently. Remember, a good friend is one who listens.

"Wow, so you must have been shocked to see the front door open!"

1. Be supportive and positive

Show empathy; even if you don't relate to their situation, try to understand and see things from their point of view. You can then be genuinely supportive and offer positive feedback. Hold back judgment and biases.

"I never had a pet, but I totally understand how devastated you were to lose yours."

1. Respect mutual friends

Once you make connections and find you have mutual friends, praise those people. Do not gossip about them. Show your new acquaintance that you have the qualities of a loyal friend.

"Oh, Sharon is a lovely person. We have known each other for ages."

1. Use emotions to conduct the conversation

If you want to add more drama to what you are saying and increase the excitement, change how you narrate stories. Don't talk about how you went to Las Vegas last weekend. Tell them how you almost won a million dollars at roulette, ended up lost in the desert, or got called up on stage to sing.

Make the other person think, "Hmm... This one is full of excitement and will be interesting to hang out with."

1. Be a loyal confidante

A person will open up to you once, and if you break their confidentiality and trust, you won't see them again. Friendship is about keeping secrets, trusting each other, and having each other's back.

"I won't say a word to anyone; I know how it feels to be analyzed."

1. Eye contact

You already know the importance of this.

1. Avoid gossiping

Never gossip with a first-time acquaintance. They may gossip back, but you will forever be remembered and branded as "that gossip." With no hope of a friendship forming because they may think you will gossip about them next.

1. Make plans for the future

If you genuinely like the other person and you have a lot in common, make an effort to explore the possibility of a friendship. Ask them if they would like to meet up for lunch or coffee, and take it from there.

"The coffee shop on the 7th is my favorite hangout; we should get together when you have the time."

1. Use social media to connect

Share account details, send out friend requests, and stay connected by following each other's activities and keeping in touch online, even if you rarely meet.

1. Don't make contacting each other a competition

I called the last time, so it's her turn next. Saying so and waiting impatiently for a call will drive a wedge in your friendship. Stop keeping score; call your friend or drop a text to say "Hi."

Looking for Common Interests and Getting to Know People

When you share similar interests and lifestyles with someone, a chemical reaction takes place that acts as a natural attraction, creating a closeness that makes conversation easier and builds rapport for long-term relationships.

In addition to the techniques we have explored thus far, use these tips to find people you can bond with as well as common ground on which to build a conversation.

- Avoid bias and judgment, look for the good, and be friendly and approachable.

If you focus on seeing the negative in a person, you will never see beyond it. You will miss signs that say they are awesome people to get to know. Therefore, focus on the good, and you will soon be enjoying a wholesome conversation. Smile readily and say "hello" to people. Make yourself approachable, and soon people will return your smiles and want to get to know you.

- Choose to socialize, explore, and make new contacts.

Don't restrict yourself to a familiar group of friends or family; choose to engage socially. Join local clubs, get involved in community work, and start a new hobby that requires mingling, like dancing, swim squads, book clubs, hiking tours, etc. Say "yes" to the next invitation to go out.

- Open up and have meaningful conversations.

Once you get past the introductions and Q&A session, be more open. Reveal a little about your personal life. I'm not asking you to give out your bank account details, but a few details that tell the other person you are comfortable with them will make them want to connect, and you can then enjoy a deep and meaningful relationship.

Deflate areas you don't agree on, change the subject, and find more amicable subjects to talk about.

- Don't set the bar too high—for yourself or others.

Don't sell yourself short and think that you are too boring or uninteresting. There are some people who avoid conversations altogether since they are under the notion that no one is interested in talking to them. Go into the conversation with the notion that you have a lot in common with the others there. I think people will be warm and welcoming. Think positively that the event you are attending will go well and that you will make new friends; tell yourself you are "excited" about the social event and not anxious.

- Don't hog the conversation.

While it's good to open up and talk about yourself, don't make it a one-sided discussion of "I, me, myself." Pause and let the other person talk. If they are too silent, ask them questions to make them talk about themselves.

Finally, Before You Can Practice Your New Techniques—Here's How to Enter a Conversation

How often have you stood on the sidelines, eavesdropping on conversations, and come up with witty answers in your head to what's being said and asked?

I'm guilty of indulging in this practice and also hopefully waiting for someone to look my way. Even if they did, they were probably confronted with my resting bitch face (I can't help it) and decided I really didn't want to be bothered. Therefore, I decided not to leave things to chance and found a method for wedging my way into a conversation.

The ARE Method

Dr. Carol Fleming introduced this method that helps with breaking into a conversation. The three points used to do so help with easy integration into an otherwise awkward situation for many introverts.

The Anchor

This is the wedge that props the door open to conversation. Use a point common to the situation to make your entry.

"I heard this helicopter tour is one of the best for aerial views of the archipelago."

"I dislike standing in line for so long just to get my morning coffee. Maybe I should get a job here, haha."

These may seem mundane comments, but they are dealing with the current situation and are good icebreakers.

The Reveal

Once you get into some small talk, start to bond with the other person. The best trick is to reveal a personal detail. Not too personal, though.

"We finally mustered the courage to take a beach holiday after getting caught in the tsunami in Thailand in 2004."

"I suffer the long lines for my coffee because I need the caffeine kick since I am not a morning person, especially since I play the sax at the blues bar every night."

The great reveal must be something that invokes curiosity in the other person and makes them ask you more questions.

Encourage

Use this step to encourage the other person to start talking about themselves, the situation, etc.

"I hear the South Pacific islands are the most beautiful; have you visited them?"

"Are you as dependent as I am on a caffeine fix, or are you here for the flavors?"

Motivate them to take the reins and continue the conversation. But if you sense they aren't too chatty, don't push it; stick to a casual flow of conversation instead.

Our final chapter sums up the entire book as we look at maintaining meaningful relationships. Enjoy conversations where you end up with a feeling of contentment and accomplishment, even if you don't remember the entire dialog. I'm talking about *having* good conversations and maintaining relationships that matter.

10

GIVING IT ALL MEANING

In the best conversations, you don't even remember what you talked about, only how it felt. It felt like we were in some place your body can't visit, some place with no ceiling and no walls and no floor and no instruments. –John Green

A ndrew met Liam at their company's regional conference, hosted in the Maldives. The two hit it off and enjoyed the exchange of information as well as having a partner with similar interests to enjoy their time in the Maldives.

Andrew headed the Hong Kong office, and Liam the Thailand branch. They loved the Maldives and visited the islands the following summer with their wives and kids. It's been three years, and the two are best of friends, visiting each other's families during vacations, supporting the other's regional branch by sending business their way, and maintaining a long-distance relationship that has extended between their spouses as well. Not only do the two families get along, but they have managed to blur the line between friends and family to cherish the bond.

What Is a Meaningful Relationship?

What Andrew and Liam enjoy are the benefits of a meaningful relationship based on mutual respect and trust. Let's look at key elements that help build and maintain such relationships, which are essential for a sense of belonging.

Strangers who turn into our closest friends are people who make us feel valued. Such friendships are established on firm foundations and are often the axis that dispels anxiety and depression to make us feel loved and needed. Such relationships are worth fighting for and worth leaving your inhibitions aside to maintain.

Here's what to look for in a quality relationship:

- Open communication, having someone to laugh and cry with.
- Honesty.
- Empathy is learning to understand the other person's needs even if you don't relate.
- Free thinking is when you are free to express your thoughts, policies, and emotions with another person.
- Dependable and supportive, knowing someone has got your back is a very self-assuring feeling.
- Purpose: A relationship must be mutually satisfying and purposeful for both parties.

Identify these qualities in a friendship, and cherish that relationship for life!

Barriers to Overcoming and Maintaining Lasting Friendships

- Technology: While we can easily connect with people via social media, we can also isolate ourselves through the same apps. A text instead of a call, video chats instead of meeting for coffee, and

Instagram updates instead of telling your best friend about your holiday in person are methods we use to stay in touch while isolating ourselves.

- A lack of empathy for others, when we are caught up in our lifestyles and struggles, makes us less focused on other people.
- Schedules that leave no time for socializing. Prioritize your to-do list, and work on the tasks that can be completed only at a specific time of the day. The rest of your time is dedicated to self-love and preservation—time with friends certainly hits the mark.
- Fearing vulnerability, we often keep people we bond with at bay for fear of getting hurt. Exposing our vulnerabilities to others can make us feel insecure, so we keep our distance from people.
- Listening to everything strangers are saying, no matter how boring, will earn you their respect and also their friendship.

Human relationships are never guaranteed to be without pain or drama, but forming connections with people has been proven to be effective against loneliness, depression, and social anxiety.

AFTERWORD

Do you still dislike small talk, or are you raring to put your new skills to the test and form lasting bonds?

I hope it's the latter because as I have helped you break down and examine every nuance that leads to overcoming your fear of social interactions, I hope that through it all, you have discovered the importance of human interactions—even for an introvert.

The rules of casual conversation are simple: listen, observe, question, and comment. Not too pushy, not too quiet, lots of empathy, and loads of confidence are the mantras I want you to live by. So, you can hold your head high and walk into that room full of strangers, ready to make your mark.

Remember this as you practice new skills:

To be yourself in a world that is constantly trying to make you something else is the greatest accomplishment. –Ralph Waldo Emerson

Please Leave a Review
I would love to hear from you. I hope you enjoyed

reading Learn How to Talk to Anyone, as much as I enjoyed putting this book together for you. I also hope it was empowering and delivered the right dose of encouragement to help you stay true to yourself and overcome your fears.

Please let me know your thoughts and views by leaving me a review.

P.S. Please visit and read the other books in this series!

BIBLIOGRAPHY

Abraham. (2018). *How Anxiety Can Impair Communication*. Calmclinic. https://www.calmclinic.com/anxiety/impairs-communication

Adams, S. (2014, November 25). *How To Convey Power With Your Voice*. Forbes. https://www.forbes.com/sites/susanadams/2014/11/25/how-to-convey-power-with-your-voice/?sh=6cfc41582e7e

Admin. (2021, November 15). *How to Find Things in Common With Anyone*. Get the Friends You Want. https://getthefriendsyouwant.com/find-things-in-common/

Ambady, N., Laplante, D., Nguyen, T., Rosenthal, R., Chaumeton, N., & Levinson, W. (2002). Surgeons' tone of voice: a clue to malpractice history. *Surgery*, *132*(1), 5–9. https://doi.org/10.1067/msy.2002.124733

Angel, D. W. (2016, December 31). *The Four Types of Conversations: Debate, Dialogue, Discourse, and Diatribe*. Medium; Medium. https://medium.com/@DavidWAngel/the-four-types-of-conversations-debate-dialogue-discourse-and-diatribe-898d19eccc0a

Anthony, R. (2017, September 17). *Communication Power of Metaphors, Analogies and Similes*. Linkedin. https://www.linkedin.com/pulse/communication-power-metaphors-analogies-similes-ray-anthony

Attitudinal Barriers To Communication: Definition, Examples and How to Overcome Attitudinal Barrier. (2021, September 8). Harappa. https://harappa.education/harappa-diaries/attitudinal-barriers-to-communication/

Barbera, L. (n.d.). *A quote by Luciano Barbera*. goodreads. Retrieved January 8, 2023, from https://www.goodreads.com/quotes/1361521-to-be-noticed-without-striving-to-be-noticed-this-is

Better Help. (2022, October 31). *How To Be More Socially Confident In Social Situations*. Betterhelp. https://www.betterhelp.com/advice/relations/how-to-feel-confident-in-awkward-social-situations/

BetterSleep. (2019, October 8). *The Vicious Cycle of Social Anxiety and Sleep*. Bettersleep. https://www.bettersleep.com/blog/vicious-cycle-of-social-anxiety-and-sleep/

BeWellLine. (n.d.). *5 Stages of Conversation: How-to Guide*. Calmhsa.org. Retrieved January 2, 2023, from https://www.calmhsa.org/wp-content/uploads/5-Stages-of-Conversation.pdf

Bongers, A., & Macartney, D. (2020). *Conversation*. Ecampusontario.pressbooks.pub. https://ecampusontario.pressbooks.pub/scientificcommunication/chapter/conversation/

Buckner, J. D., Bernert, R. A., Cromer, K. R., Joiner, T. E., & Schmidt, N. B. (2008). Social anxiety and insomnia: the mediating role of depressive symptoms. *Depression and Anxiety, 25*(2), 124–130. https://doi.org/10.1002/da.20282

Coady, L. (n.d.). *Lynn Coady Quotes*. BrainyQuote. Retrieved December 13, 2022, from https://www.brainyquote.com/quotes/lynn_coady_732362

Conversano, C., Rotondo, A., Lensi, E., Della Vista, O., Arpone, F., & Reda, M. A. (2010). Optimism and Its Impact on Mental and Physical Well-Being. *Clinical Practice & Epidemiology in Mental Health, 6*(1), 25–29. https://doi.org/10.2174/1745017901006010025

Council, F. C. (2017, October 25). *Council Post: 15 Ways You Can Find The Confidence To Speak Up*. Forbes. https://www.forbes.com/sites/forbescoachescouncil/2017/10/25/15-ways-you-can-find-the-confidence-to-speak-up/?sh=69498da317a7

Cuncic, A. (2019). *How Cognitive-Behavioral Therapy Can Treat Social Anxiety Disorder*. Verywell Mind. https://www.verywellmind.com/how-is-cbt-used-to-treat-sad-3024945

Cuncic, A. (2020a, September 19). *7 Types of Social Fears and the Best Way to Overcome Them*. Verywell Mind. https://www.verywellmind.com/practice-social-anxiety-disorder-exposure-therapy-3024845

Cuncic, A. (2020b, December 4). *5 Key Facts About Cognitive-Behavioral Group Therapy for Social Anxiety*. Verywell Mind. https://www.verywellmind.com/cognitive-behavioral-group-therapy-social-anxiety-disorder-3024944

Daubman, K. A., Heatherington, L., & Ahn, A. (1992). Gender and the self-presentation of academic achievement. *Sex Roles, 27*(3-4), 187–204. https://doi.org/10.1007/bf00290017

De Walt, J. (n.d.). *A quote by Jaeda DeWalt*. goodreads. Retrieved December 11, 2022, from https://www.goodreads.com/quotes/885113-there-are-times-i-wish-i-was-a-master-magician

Defending. (n.d.). Changingminds.org. Retrieved January 1, 2023, from http://changingminds.org/techniques/conversation/elements/defending.htm

Doyle, A. (2022, July 7). *What Are Listening Skills?* The Balance. https://www.thebalancemoney.com/types-of-listening-skills-with-examples-2063759

Dupuis, D. (n.d.). *What are the Four Listening Styles?* Mandel. https://www.mandel.com/blog/what-are-the-four-listening-styles

Edwards, V. V. (2017, March 17). *Resting Bitch Face: How to Fix Your RBF Forever (With Science)*. Science of People. https://www.scienceofpeople.com/resting-bitch-face/

Einstein, A. (n.d.). *Albert Einstein Quotes.* BrainyQuote. https://www. brainyquote.com/quotes/albert_einstein_132607

Emerson, R. W. (n.d.). *Ralph Waldo Emerson Quotes.* BrainyQuote. https://www. brainyquote.com/quotes/ralph_waldo_emerson_387459

Fivush, R. (2020, August 13). *Listening to Stories: The Power of Story Circles | Psychology Today.* Psychologytoday. https://www.psychologytoday.com/intl/ blog/the-stories-our-lives/202008/listening-stories-the-power-story-circles

Find out how food and anxiety are linked. (2017a). Mayo Clinic. https://www. mayoclinic.org/diseases-conditions/generalized-anxiety-disorder/expert- answers/coping-with-anxiety/faq-20057987

Gandhi, Y. (2022, March 20). *7 Types of Noises.* Analyticssteps. https://www. analyticssteps.com/blogs/7-types-noises

Giang, V. (2019, June 25). *7 Ways to Project Confidence With Your Body Language.* Business Trends and Insights; American Express. https://www.americanex press.com/en-us/business/trends-and-insights/articles/4-ways-your-body- language-can-project-confidence/

Gibson, C. (2016, February 2). *Scientists have discovered what causes Resting Bitch Face.* The Washington Post. https://www.washingtonpost.com/news/arts- and-entertainment/wp/2016/02/02/scientists-have-discovered-the-source- of-your-resting-bitch-face/

Goman, C. K. (n.d.). *Is Your Communication Style Dictated By Your Gender?* Forbes. Retrieved January 12, 2023, from https://www.forbes.com/sites/ carolkinseygoman/2016/03/31/is-your-communication-style-dictated-by- your-gender/?sh=141a1452eb9d

Grant, A. (n.d.). *Deeper voices earn more money.* GPB. https://www.gpb.eu/2013/ 07/deeper-voices-earn-more-money.html

Green, J. (n.d.). *A quote from Turtles All the Way Down.* goodreads. Retrieved January 13, 2023, from https://www.goodreads.com/quotes/8842654-in-the- best-conversations-you-don-t-even-remember-what-you

Gulam, K. (n.d.). *Business Communication Basic Concepts and Skills.* Uj.edu. https://www.uj.edu.sa/Files/1001210/Subjects/Chapter%205%20Listening% 20Skills%20%20.pdf

Haas, S. B. (2019). *Five Essentials to Help You Speak With More Confidence.* Psychology Today. https://www.psychologytoday.com/us/blog/prescrip tions-life/201912/five-essentials-help-you-speak-more-confidence

Harappa. (2020, September 7). *Tone of Voice: Types & Examples of Tones.* Harappa Education. https://harappa.education/harappa-diaries/tone-of- voice-types-and-examples-in-communication/

Hartley, H. (2019, June 4). *The Ultimate Guide to Confidence Building.* The Redis- covery of Me. https://rediscoveryofme.com/confidence-building/

Hartwell, M. (2016, May 17). *Turning Acquaintances Into Friends*. Psych Central. https://psychcentral.com/lib/turning-acquaintances-into-friends#1

Heather Anderson. (2019, January 14). *7 Ways to Dress Confident and Classy Yet Trendy*. Successible Life. https://successiblelife.com/7-ways-to-dress-confident-and-classy-yet-trendy/

Hendriksen, E. (2016, May 18). *The 4 Differences Between Introversion and Social Anxiety*. Quiet. https://quietrev.com/the-4-differences-between-introversion-and-social-anxiety/

Iliopoulos, A. (n.d.). *How can I get better at small talk?* Quora. Retrieved January 13, 2023, from https://www.quora.com/How-can-I-get-better-at-small-talk/answer/Adrian-Iliopoulos?ch=10&oid=18685873&share=02c5a61b&srid=h2OTRw&target_type=answer

Impact Factory. (n.d.). *The Seven Barriers to Communication*. Impact Factory. https://www.impactfactory.com/resources/the-seven-barriers-to-great-communications/

Itani, O. (2020, February 4). *4 Self-Care Morning Mantras to Boost Your Confidence*. Mind Cafe. https://medium.com/mind-cafe/4-self-care-morning-mantras-to-boost-your-confidence-3dc5daebfad7

Jain, A. (n.d.). *Aayush Jain Quotes*. Goodreads. Retrieved January 6, 2023, from https://www.goodreads.com/author/quotes/15049101.Aayush_Jain

Johnson, J. (n.d.). *The Importance of Connection through Meaningful Relationships*. Centerstone. https://centerstone.org/our-resources/health-wellness/the-importance-of-connection-through-meaningful-relationships/

Jordan, M. (n.d.). *Michael Jordan Quotes*. BrainyQuote. https://www.brainyquote.com/quotes/michael_jordan_167381

Ko, S. J., Sadler, M. S., & Galinsky, A. D. (2014). The Sound of Power. *Psychological Science, 26*(1), 3–14. https://doi.org/10.1177/0956797614553009

London Image Institute. (2019, October 14). *Key Male & Female Differences in Communication*. London Image Institute. https://londonimageinstitute.com/men-women-communication-differences/

Lumen Learning. (2019). *Lobes of the Brain | Introduction to Psychology*. Lumenlearning.com. https://courses.lumenlearning.com/waymaker-psychology/chapter/reading-parts-of-the-brain/

Magner, E. (2016, December 8). *7 tips for talking to strangers at a party*. Well and Good. https://www.wellandgood.com/how-to-talk-to-strangers-at-parties/

Martinuzzi, B. (2019, March 11). *Confident or arrogant? How to tell the difference and why it matters | Mind Tools for Business*. Mindtoolsbusiness. https://mindtoolsbusiness.com/resources/blog/confident-arrogant-difference#:~:text=That

McLay, L., Jamieson, H. A., France, K. G., & Schluter, P. J. (2021). Loneliness and social isolation are associated with sleep problems among older community-dwelling women and men with complex needs. *Scientific Reports, 11*(1). https://doi.org/10.1038/s41598-021-83778-w

Medina, S. (n.d.). *What are some common barriers to effective communication?* Quora. Retrieved January 2, 2023, from https://www.quora.com/What-are-some-common-barriers-to-effective-communication/answer/Salma-Medina-1?ch=10&oid=176659846&share=e3ab4aaf&srid=h2OTRw&target_type=answer

Menninger, K. A. (n.d.). *Karl A. Menninger Quotes.* BrainyQuote. https://www.brainyquote.com/quotes/karl_a_menninger_143978

Montgomery, S. (2020, June 23). *The Difference Between Being Boastful and Being Confident.* Stacey M Design. https://staceymdesign.com/blogs/blog/being-boastful-and-being-confident-are-not-the-same

Morin, D., & Sander, V. (2021, February 12). *23 Tips to Be Confident in a Conversation (With Examples).* SocialSelf. https://socialself.com/confident-conversation/

Morris, A. (n.d.). *Elements of the Conversation.* Changingminds.org. http://changingminds.org/techniques/conversation/elements/elements.htm

Neville, D. (n.d.). *A quote by Dorothy Nevill.* goodreads. Retrieved December 21, 2022, from https://www.goodreads.com/quotes/249912-the-real-art-of-conversation-is-not-only-to-say

Nianni. (2020, August 22). *20 POWERFUL AFFIRMATIONS TO HELP YOU STOP OVERTHINKING.* Nianni Lifestyle Blog. https://niannilifestyleblog.com/2020/08/22/20-powerful-affirmations-to-help-you-stop-overthinking/

O'Bryan, A. (2022, February 8). *How to Practice Active Listening: 16 Examples & Techniques.* Positive Psychology. https://positivepsychology.com/active-listening-techniques/

Ono, Y. (n.d.). *Yoko Ono Quotes.* BrainyQuote. Retrieved January 10, 2023, from https://www.brainyquote.com/quotes/yoko_ono_460619

Park, G., Yaden, D. B., Schwartz, H. A., Kern, M. L., Eichstaedt, J. C., Kosinski, M., Stillwell, D., Ungar, L. H., & Seligman, M. E. P. (2016). Women are Warmer but No Less Assertive than Men: Gender and Language on Facebook. *PLoS ONE, 11*(5). https://doi.org/10.1371/journal.pone.0155885

Park, S. G., & Park, K. H. (2018). Correlation between nonverbal communication and objective structured clinical examination score in medical students. *Korean Journal of Medical Education, 30*(3), 199–208. https://doi.org/10.3946/kjme.2018.94

Perini, S. J., Abbott, M. J., & Rapee, R. M. (2006). Perception of Performance as a Mediator in the Relationship Between Social Anxiety and Negative Post-Event Rumination. *Cognitive Therapy and Research, 30*(5), 645–659. https://doi.org/10.1007/s10608-006-9023-z

Phillips, M. (2018, February 23). *How to Improve Your Tonality to Quickly Build Rapport*. Medium. https://medium.com/@mvphillips18/how-to-improve-your-tonality-to-quickly-build-rapport-e2f0173e4a3c

Pocock, M. (2017, September 7). *Why Introverts Make The Best Public Speakers*. Lifehack. https://www.lifehack.org/629026/why-introverts-make-the-best-public-speakers

Psych central. (2015, April 12). *5 Tips to Improve Your Self-Talk*. Psych Central. https://psychcentral.com/blog/5-tips-to-improve-your-self-talk#4

Publisher, A. removed at the request of the original. (2016, November 8). *4.2 Listening Styles*. Open.lib.umn.edu; University of Minnesota Libraries Publishing edition, 2016. This edition is adapted from a work originally produced in 2011 by a publisher who has requested that it not receive attribution. https://open.lib.umn.edu/publicspeaking/chapter/4-2-listening-styles/

Quote. (n.d.). *Sometimes, the people you think don't want to #talk to you are the ones waiting for you to talk to them. | Talking quotes, Thinking of you, Inspirational quotes*. Pinterest. Retrieved February 3, 2023, from https://www.pinterest.co.uk/pin/485262928586471547/

Quotes. (n.d.). *Anonymous*. The Foundation for a Better Life. Retrieved January 12, 2023, from https://www.passiton.com/inspirational-quotes/7610-speak-in-such-a-way-that-others-love-to-listen

Regan, S. (2021, December 11). *The One Thing You Should Do Every Single Time You Look In The Mirror*. Mindbodygreen. https://www.mindbodygreen.com/articles/mirror-work

Rodman, S. (2014, September 2). *10 Ways To Turn a Conversation Into a Potential Friendship*. Lifehack. https://www.lifehack.org/articles/communication/10-ways-turn-conversation-into-potential-friendship.html

Ruhl, C. (2021). *What Is Cognitive Bias?* Simply Psychology. https://www.simplypsychology.org/cognitive-bias.html

Segal, J., Smith, M., Robinson, L., & Boose, G. (2020, October). *Nonverbal Communication and Body Language*. HelpGuide. https://www.helpguide.org/articles/relationships-communication/nonverbal-communication.htm

Shafir, H., M.Ed, LCMHCS, LCAS, & CCS. (2021, May 18). *How to Find Things in Common With Someone*. SocialSelf. https://socialself.com/blog/find-things-in-common/

Shukla, V. (2021, January 20). *What are Communication Barriers & How to Overcome Them- Talent Economy*. ShineLearning. https://learning.shine.com/talenteconomy/career-help/communication-barriers-and-how-to-overcome-them/

Solutions, O. W. (2020, August 11). *The Connection Between Dehydration and*

Depression | Optimum Water. Drink Optimum. https://www.drinkoptimum. com/the-connection-between-dehydration-and-depression/

Speaking in Public Speech Delivery. (n.d.). Pearsonhighered.com. Retrieved January 2023, from https://www.pearsonhighered.com/assets/samplechap ter/0/2/0/5/0205627870.pdf

Starter, J. (Teach. (2014, March 23). *5 Ls of Listening Poster.* Teach Starter. https://www.teachstarter.com/au/teaching-resource/5-ls-of-listening-poster/

Susan York Morris. (2016, July 12). *What Are the Benefits of Self-Talk?* Healthline Media. https://www.healthline.com/health/mental-health/self-talk

Swift, J. (n.d.). *Jonathan Swift Quote.* A-Z Quotes. Retrieved December 21, 2022, from https://www.azquotes.com/quote/914495

Social anxiety disorder (social phobia) - symptoms and causes. (2017b, August 29). Mayo Clinic. https://www.mayoclinic.org/diseases-conditions/social-anxi ety-disorder/symptoms-causes/syc-20353561

Tannen, D. (1995, September). *The Power of Talk: Who Gets Heard and Why.* Harvard Business Review. https://hbr.org/1995/09/the-power-of-talk-who-gets-heard-and-why

TEAM, M. T. (2018, January 19). *10 Rules of a Great Conversationalist.* MBA TUTS. https://www.mbatuts.com/10-rules-of-a-great-conversationalist/

TheTherapistAid. (2020). *Active Listening Communication Skill.* https://www. therapistaid.com/worksheets/active-listening

Thoreau, H. D. (n.d.). *Henry David Thoreau Quotes.* BrainyQuote. https://www. brainyquote.com/quotes/henry_david_thoreau_132515

Tuovinen, S., Tang, X., & Salmela-Aro, K. (2020). Introversion and Social Engagement: Scale Validation, Their Interaction, and Positive Association With Self-Esteem. *Frontiers in Psychology, 11.* https://doi.org/10.3389/fpsyg. 2020.590748

Taking Good Care of Yourself. (2022). Mental Health America. https://mhana tional.org/taking-good-care-yourself

Villiers, A. (2017, December 18). *How linguistic style can undermine perceptions of confidence.* Selection Criteria. https://www.selectioncriteria.com.au/job-interviews/linguistic-style-can-undermine-perceptions-confidence/

Wang, Y., Chen, J., Zhang, X., Lin, X., Sun, Y., Wang, N., Wang, J., & Luo, F. (2022). The Relationship between Perfectionism and Social Anxiety: A Moderated Mediation Model. *International Journal of Environmental Research and Public Health, 19*(19), 12934. https://doi.org/10.3390/ijerph191912934

Water Science School. (2019, May 22). *The Water in You: Water and the Human Body | U.S. Geological Survey.* usgs.gov. https://www.usgs.gov/special-topics/ water-science-school/science/water-you-water-and-human-body

Waters. (2021, September 20). *How to read body language and gain deeper emotional awareness.* Betterup. https://www.betterup.com/blog/how-to-read-body-language

What The Pinoy. (2019, March 2). *How do I get better at carrying conversations?* Reddit. https://www.reddit.com/r/socialskills/comments/awflef/how_do_i_get_better_at_carrying_conversations/?utm_source=share&utm_medium=web2x&context=3

Wilde, O. (n.d.). *Oscar Wilde Quotes.* BrainyQuote. Retrieved January 2, 2023, from https://www.brainyquote.com/quotes/oscar_wilde_109875

Wittgenstein, L. (n.d.). *Ludwig Wittgenstein Quotes.* BrainyQuote. Retrieved January 10, 2023, from https://www.brainyquote.com/quotes/ludwig_wittgenstein_139240

Zauderer, S. (2022, December 6). *31 Fear Of Public Speaking Statistics (Prevalence).* Crossrivertherapy. https://www.crossrivertherapy.com/public-speaking-statistics

Zetlin, M. (2016, May 4). *21 common body language mistakes even smart people make.* Business Insider. https://www.businessinsider.com/21-common-body-language-mistakes-even-smart-people-make-2016-4#-20

Made in the USA
Las Vegas, NV
05 March 2024

86758056R00085